SHOW ME COLOUR

Show Me Colour: Notes on love, loss, grief and renewal
By Rosalind Gibb
Published by Citadel Books
www.rosalindgibb.com

ISBN 978-0-9931142-0-5

Copyright © Rosalind Gibb 2014

Some names have been changed in Part 2.

Show Me Colour
Notes on love, loss, grief and renewal

Rosalind Gibb

Citadel Books

PART 1

And did you get what you wanted from this life, even so?
I did.
And what did you want?
To call myself beloved, to feel myself beloved on the earth.

Raymond Carver

SUMMER HARVEST

For a time I would have worn a T-shirt emblazoned with *I ♥ Carlisle*, had one existed, which I don't think it did because to most people Carlisle is an anonymous city off the M6, known as somewhere you change trains and for being mentioned in a song by The Smiths.

I'd never been until I attended an interview for a job (as a feature writer at the local newspaper), yet got such a warm feeling about the place I knew I wanted to live there.

As soon as I stepped out of the station I took to the place: its red brick buildings, factories, textile mills and railway lines; permanent reminders of a gloriously industrious past. Towering Dixon's Chimney – the one skyline icon – amid wide skies which could change from blue to grey in seconds.

When I moved there, in 2008, it was resolutely uncosmopolitan, like stepping back into the 1980s.

The main music venue was the leisure centre (with a plaque recording the grand opening by Neil Kinnock). Restaurants still had stiff table linen and pastel-coloured carpets, cafés that sold scones and prawn salads outnumbered coffee chains offering overpriced lattes and panini, and when a Nando's arrived it was front page news.

But Carlisle had – and still has – an unpretentiousness, a realness, that appealed to me. Large chains had not ripped the heart out of the city centre and you were – and still are – pretty much guaranteed a warm welcome (and reasonable prices) in shops, bars and restaurants.

After years living in Edinburgh and London this seemed a remarkable thing.

Then there were the people, who always make a place. It's the only city I've worked in where passers-by not only readily agree to do vox pops for the local paper, but stand and chat with you afterwards.

A Cumbrian combo I frequently encountered was a steely core crossed with a big-heartedness. I soon saw that most Cumbrians don't take any bullshit but they'd do anything to help you.

It's a brilliant, honest balance and one aptly echoed in the Carlisle motto: *Be Just and Fear Not*, which is displayed outside historic buildings, on street signs and set into pavement mosaics.

A civic pride subtly etched into the city's conscience and instilled in almost everyone I met.

For these reasons and many more I loved living in Carlisle. It had taken a few years to get there, but at the age of 35 I could truthfully say that life was good and I was happy. Then, suddenly, unexpectedly, it got even better.

I'd known Andrew for around six years, at first as a colleague and acquaintance, then as a valued friend. We chatted regularly by text and I'd meet him for a coffee on visits back to Edinburgh.

I invited him to visit Carlisle for a weekend, as I enjoyed his company and suspected he would also appreciate the city. And one weekend in April 2010, everything changed.

Anyone who's fallen in love with someone where

there's already an established friendship knows how deeply it's felt. After all, you're friends for genuine reasons: you make each other laugh, you're there to chat to, you find each other interesting, you respect each other. Suddenly, for whatever mystery reason, you see each other in a new, magical light. We soon got over any amusing awkwardness, in that switch from friends to girlfriend and boyfriend.

And then we had the best time.

If there was a word to describe our time together I'd choose abundance. Not a material, tangible abundance but something felt in your soul and in your heart. Life had suddenly become infused with thrills and sparks and goodness and we each now had a hand to hold, through easy days and tougher days.

Andrew had an infectious lust for life, a wonderfully enquiring mind and the kindest heart. And I'd never met anyone who made me laugh so much. All in all a perfect combination. I felt like the luckiest girl in the world.

I didn't even tell many people about it, not in much detail anyway. I'm sure that would have come but there was no need for outside validation. We knew what we had and, as our feelings blossomed, how special it felt.

Because we lived in different places (he lived in Musselburgh, a few miles east of Edinburgh) we spoke on the phone and those long calls became the highlight of my day, supplemented by frequent texts. In these days of sporadic email communication it felt so good to talk and laugh, properly, in real time. Not to mention having a kindred spirit when it came to texts – we both often wrote so much that it had to be sent in two or three messages.

We aimed to see each other most weekends and cherished our time together. We had enough experience under our belts to know what we were doing and what we wanted, in and out of bed. We relished late nights and long lies, and experienced that sad but excited feeling saying goodbye on a Sunday night.

Apart from having to make that last train, we lived in our own time zone, as you do during those early loved-up days.

We decided to call each other by our Sunday names. He had all kinds of monikers from different eras of his life. I'm known by my family as Rozzi and lots of people call me Ros. During our friendship Andrew had called me Rosalind and vice versa. We liked it and it stuck – sort of nicknames in reverse.

We chatted animatedly, often about nonsensical things yet it all made perfect sense, and we laughed a lot. We drew each other pictures, took tours of Carlisle, admiring its gems and idiosyncrasies, and ate ice creams in the sunshine (double scoops mandatory). We watched schlock horror films, ate Chinese takeaways, had afternoon snoozes and talked and talked about past experiences, current states of affairs, future hopes and wants.

The latter became more prevalent as the weeks passed, once autumn arrived and it was clear that this was so much more than a summer fling.

Those few months together were beautiful and I wouldn't change any of it, even knowing now what was to happen next.

AUTUMN HORROR

One Sunday in mid-October we spent most of the day in bed and made a pact: while we were living in different cities, every Sunday we were together would be spent as a proper lazy day.

No getting up early, making ourselves go out for walks or day trips, just to supposedly make the most of the weekend. For now we had everything we needed right here, just the two of us. I felt like I could have stayed there forever.

It was dark and raining hard as we walked to the station for his train. We kissed farewell on the grey bridge scarred with chewing gum splats, and I felt that pang of sadness, knowing I'd miss him.

"I'll call you later," Andrew said in his gentle voice as he walked away, cheeks flushed and a smile crossing his face. He turned the corner to walk down the steps and already I couldn't wait to see him again.

Over the next two weeks we talked on the phone and texted and counted the sleeps until we would be together again, like a pair of excited kids.

Now, in this last week of October 2010, there was just one sleep until our trip to Blackpool – our first romantic weekend away and a belated birthday celebration for Andrew, who had turned 45 on the Tuesday.

The day before our trip, on the Thursday, I sent him a

5

jokey text asking if he'd packed yet. I didn't hear anything back (normally he'd reply quickly, excitedly) but assumed he was out at the cinema or meeting a friend.

After work I thought it strange that he hadn't been in touch at all. I phoned him and after his amusingly blunt voicemail message, in that lovely Cockney accent, I left a message asking him to call.

I phoned about an hour later. Voicemail again. Strange, but perhaps he was at a double bill.

I went to a friend's house for tea and left my phone at my flat, to stop me checking it every two minutes and experiencing that sinking feeling when there were no new messages.

On the way I wondered if he'd bailed out because he suddenly didn't like the idea of us being together. It happens, but here it didn't make sense. That would mean I'd imagined our connection and I was certain I hadn't, though it's funny just how much you can start to question things when a seed of doubt is planted.

But more than that: if Andrew *was* having second thoughts about where we were heading relationship-wise, I knew he was the type of person to communicate about it. He wouldn't have just ignored my calls and texts. No way.

I got back to my flat at around 9pm and looked at my phone. No new messages. My heart sank but in a different way this time. I phoned his mobile again. Voicemail.

Then I remembered Facebook. I logged on, telling myself that if Andrew had updated his status in the last few hours, then he was okay.

I saw he had posted a link to his website, Bank Holiday Britain, that morning. There was a moment of relief, then a hollowness in my stomach. If he'd been on Facebook, why hadn't been answering his phone? Where was he?

There was something wrong. I felt it. I imagined him at his flat, where he lived alone, and thought perhaps he had had an accident. But how could I get there now? The trains had stopped running and I didn't have a car. What would I do when I got there? Bang on his door? Randomly visit different hospitals?

My mind was racing. I started to pack, then of all things, I started ironing. I detest ironing but, now, it was a robotic distraction from the panicky butterflies swooshing round my stomach, and one part of my mind trying to reassure the other that it would all turn out to be fine.

It was no good. I soon gave up. I sat on my bed and cried, knowing that the only way of finding out how Andrew was, was through his mobile phone.

It was my only method of contacting him, which now seemed so ludicrous. I hadn't met his family, didn't really know his friends, knew he was on holiday from work so wouldn't have been due in there anyway.

I started feeling claustrophobic and helpless. Could Facebook give me one more reassurance?

I don't know how much time had passed, but I logged on again and saw a mutual friend's status, paying tribute to Andrew. I blinked as though I'd just hallucinated and looked again. But this must be another Andrew he knows, right?!! I logged out, as though I'd merely seen a photo of a cute cat or some such, and walked into my living room.

Everything was blurry and out of sync as my heartbeat got faster and louder and my breathing quickened.

I paced up and down, not wanting to stop, refusing to acknowledge what I had just read.

(People said, in the weeks after, that learning of Andrew's death on Facebook must have been one of the worst ways to find out. But I'm not sure there's a 'better' way. A police officer arriving at your door, a telegram with news of a death on the Front, even a relative telling you the worst thing in the world has happened... no matter the medium, surely nothing can make the news of a sudden death any easier. Nothing at all.)

I needed confirmation it had not happened and phoned an old friend in Edinburgh who worked in the same building as Andrew.

He started crying as soon as he answered, as I said in a perky voice, as though it was a perfectly normal phone call: "I'm trying to find Andrew...", hoping against hope the reply would be: "Yes, I've just been in the pub with him! His phone was stolen but he's around. He's fine!"

Instead he said through his tears: "I shouldn't be telling you this..."

The light (reality?) dimmed and the sound changed, like when your hearing goes echoey after a plane journey. I paced up and down my living room, picturing Andrew in a blue jumper (which I'd only seen him wear once), like a framed photo of him. That was him in the past. In the present, I was thinking *We're going to Blackpool tomorrow, it'll all be alright.* This second thought battled with the first; active denial fighting fact, a fact too massive and too devastating to be allowed to win.

"Your sisters are on their way. They are on their way to yours now," my friend was saying, clearly and slowly.

And it was only then I grasped something. After roughly a day of missed calls, unanswered texts and voicemail messages; of thinking he'd had an accident or a health scare and picturing seeing him in a hospital bed and shouting at him for not being in touch (proof, if it were needed, of just how much I cared about him); of speaking to my friend, who was crying at this shocking news of his acquaintance's death – after all of this it was those six words that hit home somewhere in my befuddled brain.

"Your sisters are on their way."

I pondered this. That meant travelling some 100 miles from Edinburgh. Leaving their families, young children, partners, jobs, homes, in a rush and without arranging it in advance.

I knew this meant the situation was gravely serious, but it was all happening in another world I hadn't got to yet.

So instead I stared at my suitcase in the hall and thought *I'll see Andrew tomorrow. He wouldn't abandon me just like that!*

I wished he was here, now, wrapping me in his strong arms and kissing me hello. And then my flat buzzer rang and I heard my twin sister's voice.

The explanation – a heart attack at the gym – was so alien it sounded like a foreign phrase. Everything felt like an out-of-body experience, like being in a film or a book at exactly the same time as watching or reading it.

I prayed there was an end, a final page, when it was revealed that Andrew hadn't died and it had been a case of mistaken identity. A lame plot twist, granted, but one I would have given anything to read.

I remember I didn't want to sit down. That it felt like someone was tapping me on the shoulder to explain what was happening, but I couldn't turn around to face the truth.

I couldn't think of one single memory of Andrew because if I thought of even one it would be like opening floodgates, which could then never be closed, and I'd think of them all. And the idea that there were no more memories to be made with Andrew was simply too painful. I could not have survived had I followed that thought process.

There were reminders everywhere of course. I had made up a party bag of goodies for a Blackpool treat which stayed on my living room table for months afterwards. I couldn't bear to move it, to cut that tie with the past and should-have-been future.

I didn't want to go out, then I felt claustrophobic and couldn't stay indoors. We went for a walk round the block and I remember the crunch of autumn leaves being more audible than my sisters' occasional conversation.

That first night three words rang through my head. *You just do.* I'd heard this or a variation on it many times in my job as a features writer. During interviews people would tell me about tragedies, of losing loved ones, often suddenly and unexpectedly. I'd ask how they got through something that sounded so impossible – curious as a fellow human being as well as a journalist – and the answer was always the same.

Now, with a broken heart and a life shattered into pieces, I clung onto these words, desperate for some hope, however distant. *You just do.*

I suddenly felt exhausted and slept for an hour or two, possibly even blacked out, then woke with a start and sat bolt upright.

My sisters (I have four siblings and my twin sister and middle sister had come down from Edinburgh) were taking turns to watch over me. One of them came over and offered me a homeopathic remedy and I drifted off into a half sleep to the strains of random through-the-night TV. Pure silence was too scary a prospect.

The next morning, as I opened my eyes and the room slowly spun into focus, I felt dizzy and confused. My throat was dry and my head hurt. "I should be in the hotel room in Blackpool," I sobbed. "Not here! We should be together there!" I didn't understand what was happening. Was I dreaming? Then I thought I was going to throw up.

In the beginning I simply kept existing. Not living, just existing. Getting out of bed. Remembering to eat. Concentrating on the day, minute to minute. Then, gradually, hour to hour. In time the tasks would become more advanced; making a cup of tea or arranging to meet a friend for a coffee.

Oftentimes I longed to take a pill that would make me sleep for ages and ages, and wake up only when it was all over. But I knew deep down there was no magic end point and the only option was to go through it all, through the searing pain, and find a path to some kind of healing.

Sudden deaths happen all the time, of course, yet it is the most isolating experience. I wrestled with this odd combination of facts in the months to come.

Perhaps because I am a writer, almost instantly I had an urge to read about grief. I needed a reference point with information telling me it had happened before and that people had survived it. I couldn't fathom how anyone could have got through this nightmare, but perhaps words in print would offer some proof they had.

My sisters went into town and returned with a selection of books including a collection of poems and quotes written over the centuries, religious and non-religious, several of which I found a great comfort in the months to come. That first day I looked through it and came across this:

When you are sorrowful look again in your heart, and you shall see that in truth you are weeping for that which has been your delight. – Kahil Gibran.

It struck such a chord with me. I stared at the words for ages in a kind of hypnosis, as fat tears fell on the fresh white pages.

The shock meant I didn't really sleep for days, and for the first three or so weeks my mind shut down and worked like an anaesthetic.

I couldn't do basic tasks like lock my front door and I had to concentrate on walking in a straight line as I left the house. But it meant my mind was numbed to this wholly unexpected and unwanted reality.

Mid-afternoon every day I'd get dizzy and my legs would turn to jelly. I physically could not keep standing and would have to go and lie down. No sleeping drugs required; my mind simply knocked me out for around an hour each time, like clockwork. It was so powerful I marvelled at it, even in my zombie state.

This foggy limbo was intersected with sudden moments of sharp clarity. But for most of that time I was so vulnerable that I reverted to being like a helpless child.

I relied on people providing food, water, medicine; answering calls and texts; driving me places or accompanying me outside for some fresh air.

I even vaguely recall my twin sister tying my shoelaces for me when we were out for a walk. The first time I saw my eldest sister after Andrew's death she gave me a hug, and as I cried she gently cradled the back of my head, the way you do when holding a newborn baby.

I could not cope with practical everyday tasks, yet I managed the trip from Carlisle to Edinburgh, not once but twice. First, to meet Andrew's parents and view his body, and then for his funeral, a blur containing moments of beauty.

I had been longing to see my sweetheart again and here he was, stone cold dead in a room in a funeral parlour. It was a dark, austere place (as you'd expect I suppose) with high ceilings and tall windows, though the only view was trees blowing against a grey autumn sky.

I told the receptionist who I was there to see, and sat patiently on a wooden bench at the side of the staircase, as though I was waiting to attend a job interview.

I remember going into the room like you remember seeing a film; a kind of secondary experience that you observe but are not quite part of. I jumped when I saw him. I wondered if he was going to spring up and forwards like some comically ghoulish marionette and say it was all a joke. I stood next to him, rooted to the spot, the odd judder coursing through my body.

It turned out some clichés you hear about death are true (isn't that why clichés exist?). As the initial fear passed, I studied him and thought he looked peaceful, like he was asleep. But also like a waxwork version of himself.

The body had been a vessel for Andrew's soul and spirit and it was clear these had left long ago. Where had they gone? I didn't believe in god or an afterlife but found myself looking up, not down.

I'd seen many times, in films and TV programmes, people being shown the body of a loved one and breaking down in hysterics there and then. In real life shock takes over so the reality of the situation doesn't sink in all at once. If it did, what would be the point in continuing to live?

(The only realistic depiction I've seen is in the original Danish version of *The Killing*. In the weeks after their daughter is murdered, the mum and dad don't break down in tears at conveniently regular intervals. Instead they brilliantly portray the raw horror; robotically getting through the day, wearing confused, haunted expressions as they try their damnedest to continue with life. It is subtle and graceful, and some of the best acting I've ever seen.)

I stayed with Andrew for perhaps another minute, standing close to his body and gently rocking myself backwards and forwards, as though I was trying to hold my balance.

I looked up to the ceiling, beyond this building and to a place I imagined he now was. I pictured him munching one of his favourite sweets, Raspberry Ruffles, in a park. Or at the beach? He would surely be somewhere outdoors anyway, walking or sitting and watching the world go by, taking photos with one of his cameras perhaps.

I kissed his forehead, looked up and whispered: "Thank you for everything."

It was one of the hardest things I did but necessary because I didn't believe it had happened (and wouldn't in the months to come). That is until I pictured his body, witnessed with my own eyes. Peaceful, still and no longer him.

You expect to meet a new boyfriend's parents over Sunday lunch or at a family birthday perhaps. I first met Andrew's parents at his flat in Musselburgh, two days after he had walked out of it, never to return. Straight away I learned they were lovely people. His brother and sister-in-law too. Kind, open, funny and with a mass of unconditional love for Andrew, their support and their generous spirits helped carry me through those first months and beyond, and it's something for which I'll forever be grateful.

They were sorting through Andrew's belongings those

first few days, and with so many possessions still in their respective places (car boot sale finds in the kitchen cupboards, trainers next to the sofa, cat litter trays in the hall cupboard, clothes in the wardrobe) I fully expected him to breeze through the front door any minute.

After being chaperoned everywhere for the first few days I had started doing things for myself, like going to the shops. But when I went to buy shoes for the funeral (even now that sentence sounds surreal – and not least because I hate shoe shopping) I took a friend, unsure if I could complete this transaction myself.

The salespeople's high-pitched patter – "Are you buying them for anything nice?" – struck somewhere but then ricocheted off me and back into day to day life, where I was not really present.

This happened a lot. And sometimes it would be a lovely moment. When I bought Raspberry Ruffles for the funeral goodie bags I asked for around a jar and a half's worth, which flustered the sweetie shop owner a little.

"Well..." he smiled sheepishly, "These must be for someone very special."

"Yes," I replied in a haze. "They are."

One day before the funeral I spent most of the afternoon lying on my twin sister's sofa in Edinburgh, gazing out at the dusky purplish sky, her greyhound Lucy by my side.

Oh how I love that dog! She'd lie at my feet and place

her chin or a paw on me, bringing a calm presence. She would sometimes do crazy jumps in the morning, her flailing limbs and her awkward, manic grin always making me smile, even now.

There was a mobile hanging from the ceiling and I lay there, listening to Lucy's occasional sighs as she relaxed, and watching the mobile gently swing from side to side.

I would lurch from having racing thoughts and the question with no answer (*why has this happened?*) spinning around my head, to this kind of meditative state. I'd find myself being strongly drawn to something – a painting, wildlife or a photo – and study it for ages.

On a train back to Carlisle that winter we got delayed near Gretna. I was starting to panic, having visions of being stuck there for hours. Then a murmuration of starlings appeared in the sky, their en masse swooping blackness a sight to behold, and one I'd always wanted to see. I watched it for several minutes, bewitched by this wonder of nature.

The day after the funeral my twin sister and I walked along a beach in East Lothian. It was a gloriously, inappropriately sunny day and I was desperately trying to think of good things, of some kind of sanity in this madness.

Not to pretend it hadn't happened and all was fine, but more for some kind of crutch to help me keep going. Because, really, all I desired was to walk into the flat calm sea and keep walking and walking into oblivion.

Then my body reminded me where I was. There was a

heaviness in my legs, like I'd been walking uphill for hours, and I felt so tired I just wanted to be indoors and lie down and never get up again.

Normally Lucy would run across the beach but she stayed at our pace, walking alongside us protectively. I said I needed to leave, and when we got back I lay down in my sister's bedroom and passed out for an hour. The anaesthetic working its wonders again.

When I woke up I lay there and realised, for the first time in days, that I was hungry. I sloped downstairs and took a bite of a sandwich. It was shop-bought, ham and mustard, nothing special.

Then an unexpected thing happened: I tasted the tang of mustard on my tongue and it was the most delicious thing in the world. A powerful energy surged through me and I realised: *I'm here. I don't know why or how, but I'm still here.*

WINTER MADNESS

Experiencing a sudden bereavement for the first time means being spectacularly unequipped to deal with the aftermath.

No experience to draw on or tools to use. Much of it is a guessing game, like stumbling through the dark. All those *you just do* people hadn't said how they'd got through it, only that they had.

When I returned to my flat in Carlisle after the first trip to Edinburgh, I went to bed as normal, if only because this was my life for the foreseeable future and I didn't know what other option there was. Besides, a decent sleep could be beneficial, or so my logical mind told me.

But during the night I woke up in the pitch black and felt more frightened than ever. I knew immediately something was wrong, but in those first few seconds I couldn't remember what and panicky thoughts raced through my mind. My heart was pounding, I felt clammy and so dizzy I thought I was going to pass out.

From the very early days my instinct had told me to move with my grief, and I think that was one of the only times I consciously tried to bury it, to keep calm and carry on – and my reaction spoke volumes.

So I made a pact with myself: to try to go with my feelings, whatever they were. Easier said than done, of course, especially for grief novices, but the pact at least felt right. And ever since that night, and for at least a year after, I slept with the light on so I knew as soon as I woke up that life had changed forever.

Early on I made the decision to go through it all, and I mean right through the middle of that scary, vast, black lagoon of grief.

While people are there with love and support – and I was lucky to have caring family and friends – they cannot change the situation.

I hoped for a miracle that it hadn't happened (my journal entries over the first few months are scattered with pleas for it not to have) but it had. No-one could turn the clock back, no matter how much I – or they – wished they could.

I also knew deep down that many people would soon forget about it, once the drama had stopped. Unless you are directly involved, unless you *feel* it, over time other things will naturally take precedence.

So it was going to be a long journey, and solitary too. The one person who would have held my hand through everything was not here. And this thought (which had not yet become my reality) made my head hurt and filled me with an emptiness.

I'd never known a loneliness like it; fierce and untamed and, as it would transpire, always there. Either in the foreground, swirling around my body and pounding through my head, making me feel seasick. Or in the background, more subtle but making me feel out of sync and slightly anxious. But whatever the guise, it didn't ever dissipate.

In those early days I'd sit on my bed and look up at the ceiling and ask whoever could hear me why Andrew had gone. Why now? And why *him*? Why this funny, kind, singular person who gave so much pleasure to people and had *lived* life, not simply let it pass him by?

Other days I thought that if I walked into town he would be there, sitting on what we had called our rendezvous bench, the place we always met on a Friday teatime.

And I had got so used to telling Andrew about everything, about day to day happenings and bigger thoughts and dreams, I frequently had an urge to text him; to tell him about seeing his body, what his funeral was like, or just how the day had gone.

I understand it's hard for people to know what to say following a sudden loss, or whether what you say will be the 'right' thing. But is there any right thing to say in this most wrong of situations?

I heard many times of people being worried about coming out with something clichéd, inappropriate or trite. But I honestly found words, any words, better than none.

Also, as a natural optimist, I was receptive to people telling me things that gave me hope. If everyone had simply said: "This is the most terrible thing in the world. There is nothing I can say to make you feel better," I really would have had no reason to keep going.

When I met good friends for the first time after Andrew's death, I told them I was okay to talk about it and they could ask me anything. It had been immediately clear to me that it had to be talked about.

Indeed I told them quite matter-of-factly, in my dazed state and with few or no tears, about the sequence of events the night it happened. I never tired of retelling the same, detailed story. A way of processing the shock I suppose.

I valued reading texts and cards, especially ones with long, thoughtful messages, and meeting family members and friends who were positive and interested and brave enough to be by my side as I moved through my grief.

My dear, thoughtful mum had always written me letters when I'd lived away and now sent them once or twice a week, mixing into her usual chitchat some pearls of wisdom. One of them I found so useful I wrote it out in my journal, and as I did so heard her speaking the simple, nurturing words:

"In the end it's only time that will really make you feel better. It's like a medicine – you keep taking it because you know it will cure you, even if there's no obvious improvement right away. Time's the same, except you don't need to take it, it's carrying on anyway. And although you won't be feeling it working yet, it is doing its job, slowly but surely, and eventually you'll be fine again. You just have to believe it, so you know in the future you will be okay."

As the shock wears off, grief feels like a madness. And yet it is a sane, natural reaction to this most stark and nonsensical of experiences. It helps us process the loss and, in time, heal.

There's a whole new raft of feelings. I thought it was strange that my broken heart didn't hurt, in a physical sense. But it sent signals to other parts of my body.

I frequently had a knotted stomach and spinning head. I felt nauseous though rarely threw up – I was too empty for that. I'd have a headache for days on end. It didn't develop into anything dramatic like a migraine, just a constant dull pain that was there when I went to bed and there when I woke up.

I was homesick a couple of times on sleepovers as a child, and then once when I was 25 and arrived in a hostel room in Prague, after spending a fun weekend with a friend in Amsterdam and on the start of my solo inter-railing trip.

It took me by surprise but there was no doubt what it was; that hollow feeling in my tummy. I felt I was about five years old again and just wanted my mum, so instead went for a beer with an Australian who was in my dorm. Listening to her talk all night seemed preferable to my temporary loneliness.

Now I felt those pangs even though I was at home. I didn't want to be here. I wanted to be back in the world I knew, with Andrew. There was nowhere to go to cure this, a permanent homesickness, and sometimes I'd double over and hold my stomach as it felt like a real, physical pain.

I frequently clutched at a necklace I wore. It was gold, heart-shaped, with a falcon on it. I had bought it long before I got together with Andrew.

I remember him admiring it and I wore it while I was with him, so it reminded me of happy times. In the months after his death I didn't take it off. I'd instinctively clutch at it, using it like some kind of comfort blanket.

On top of the physical stuff there's the crazy, exhausting ride of emotions, where you're struck down by incomprehension, an overwhelming fear and a heavy melancholia and, at times, lifted by an enormous burst of adrenaline.

And the more abstract feelings: socialising with friends and feeling a million miles away, dreams of being reunited with your lover. One day I looked in the mirror and the image started going blurry. I laughed in disbelief; I didn't know who I was any more.

I was in a constantly heightened state and at the same time felt like I was locked in a room or stuck in a lift. Some place where I did not want to be, but no-one could come to the rescue.

I often felt frozen, in both a physical and emotional sense, unable to move backwards and too afraid to move forwards.

Being overwhelmed by grief all day and all night would be too much for any human being to endure, so it comes in waves. Intense waves, completely terrifying at first and it's hard to see how you will get through it. But you do.

Sometimes I tried to take a wave head on and ride it but other days I collapsed under it and lay flat, feeling crushed and breathless from crying and so scared that this was life now, set in stone.

After the first few times, to ease the scariness (because each wave was as scary as the last), I thought a simple mantra: *This too shall pass. All things must pass.*

Anyone who's lost a partner suddenly will surely know these feelings. Anyone who hasn't couldn't possibly understand – something I had to keep in mind when I hated everyone for letting me feel so completely alone.

One night, staying at my middle sister's house, I woke from a fitful sleep and saw unidentified shapes flying through the darkness and then Andrew, there in the room and wearing red. "Why did you go? Why did you have to go?" I asked. He did not answer.

Later, and not for the first time, I lamented to my sister: "I don't want this to have happened!" and she replied that she understood, adding: "Believe me, if any of us could change it, we would."

And I realised that it was out of anyone's control. In future months when I got angry with people leading what looked like perfect lives – that is, their partner was alive and well – I remembered that comment. It wasn't just me who didn't want it to have happened. No-one did.

Some days I saw Andrew in shops, on buses and in cafés. In crowded places I paced ahead of people of a similar height or gait, just to see them head on and check they weren't him. If they were with a partner I felt angry. Why were they allowed to enjoy a long life together?

Around two days before the first anniversary of Andrew's death I had unintentionally left the living room light on when I went out to work.

When I opened the door that evening I smiled, fully expecting to see him there. *He's come back! He didn't leave!* I thought, rushing inside. As I shut the door reality swung back into focus … the flat was empty and I felt a surge of loneliness.

I sank down to the floor in my hall and cried. Partly because I missed him so much but also because the experience frightened me. A full year after it had happened, I really believed his death had all been a dream. One year on and I still felt like I was going insane.

I dreamt frequently that Andrew was still alive. Of all the moments, the one I hated most was those few seconds just after waking and thinking all was fine, then being hit by reality.

In most of the dreams we'd be reunited and I'd feel deliriously happy. Occasionally there would be a time limit. "You have 10 minutes ... five minutes," an anonymous person would tell us, like an announcer on a boating lake. "Come in, boat number 12!"

Sometimes I'd say to other people in the dream: "You see! This is why I thought about him so much, because I knew I'd see him again!"

In one dream I saw Andrew's body in a morgue under a blanket and he suddenly jumped up. It was terrifying. When I told the doctor in the dream about it (who had had his back turned) he said I'd imagined it.

On Christmas Eve I dreamt I was searching for Andrew with his mum and dad – but we were told he had become a spy with a new identity so he could never contact us again, as ordered by MI5. I was actually quite impressed when I woke from that one, and the fact that my brain had added an exotic twist for Christmas Day.

Even after brutally sudden deaths there are happy times too. It should, logically, be inherently bleak but of course our heart and our spirit do not exist on logic.

I had moments when I loved thinking of our time together, even in the knowledge it would always now be in the past. We'd been in an exciting, tantalising, sensual relationship and those feelings do not just disappear.

We were still getting to know each other but in a way this added to the beauty; there was a spontaneity to everything. Each conversation and experience was cloaked in a honeymoon magic.

I have no memories of dull discussions about washing up, or arguments, or of being bored of each other. I didn't really question when that would have come, or what it would have been like, for it had all been lived and enjoyed in the moment.

And it was the hardest thing, having that stolen away. Why had we not been given years together like other couples?

Yet on another level I took comfort from the way it ended. If any of us got to choose how to leave this earth, wouldn't we opt for it to be fast and free of a long, painful, debilitating illness or a shutting down of the mind? And wouldn't we wish to feel a true happiness on our final day?

And then there were the funny, surreal moments during those early days. I laughed a lot with my sisters and his family. I heard phrases or words being used that Andrew would have giggled at and looked up to the ceiling or sky and repeated them to him. Was he there? Could he see us?

When my twin sister phoned one day at around noon I was sitting in my dressing gown, absent-mindedly flicking through TV channels. She asked what I was up to.

"I'm watching the Dog Channel," I said nonchalantly. "I mean the God Channel."

"Is somebody with you?" she asked in a concerned voice, clearly wondering if this was the moment I had gone past the point of no return.

On the first drive up to Edinburgh with my sisters, to see my family and meet his, we missed the exit from the motorway and ended up driving through villages in Lanarkshire we'd never heard of.

They had odd names and a *Truman Show* feel about them (or more probably my whole world did). As people walked along the main street with buggies and dogs, past butchers and bakers, postboxes and phone kiosks, I expected them to turn the corner and off the stage set, with the director standing there holding his clipboard and shouting "Cut!".

We stopped for tea at a pub on the outskirts of Edinburgh and giggled throughout our meal. We'd barely slept for nights on end and our surreal situation was so at odds with this most ordinary of venues, full of families out for a Saturday evening meal. And yes, three days after Andrew died I gobbled up a whole portion of fish and chips. He would have been proud.

The rawness means everything is heightened and when good moments strike they feel wonderful. Landscapes, buildings, trees, flowers and even conversations can take on a new dimension, like life has been spiked with LSD.

Just before the funeral it was a beautiful day, calm and sunny, and I walked along Portobello Beach. I strode across the sand and felt truly grateful for all the moments we had shared.

Everything had a sharpness to it. The golden sand, the glistening sea, boats in the distance and the endless sky. I wanted to stay in this place forever.

It was interesting, knowing at this early stage that these were final memories, because so many times after that I thought Andrew was still alive. It was like part of my mind was ahead of the rest of it.

I liked these happy memories, there was a comfort to them, and so I kept walking, all the way along the beach, through Seafield and across Leith Links, up Easter Road and then through Holyrood Park, round Arthur's Seat and back to Portobello through Duddingston.

Miles and miles and miles. I didn't want to stop, to leave that place of peace. I read, in the months to come, about many instances of grieving people having a strong desire to walk and walk and, yes, some days it makes perfect sense.

On occasion friends instructed me not to feel guilty about enjoying myself and feeling good. But I never did. It made sense that extreme highs would follow extreme lows; that an intense happiness could be at the other side of a crashing wave of sadness and fear. Andrew would have been pleased I had some respite, I'm sure of that.

Plus I experienced moments of wonderful lucidity and a oneness with the world I'll never forget.

Around three weeks after Andrew's death I returned to the real world and work, and to the harsh realisation that in British culture death is still a massive taboo.

The open conversations about life and death I'd had with close friends while off work had felt so right, and I reckoned it could be helpful to see other people and get back to my job. Forward steps.

But that first day back, when I'd had to ask my boss to meet me at reception because I was so frightened about returning, was a disaster.

A couple of colleagues who brought mail or back-to-work forms to my desk said something (along the lines of "It's good to see you back"), but only one colleague in the entire open-plan office came over with the specific purpose of asking how I was.

People looked frightened when they saw me, as though the Grim Reaper would jump out from behind and capture them, a look I got many times in the months to come when I mentioned Andrew's name.

I guess they didn't know what to say, or assumed I wanted to get on with life (three weeks later! That would be some miracle). Or maybe they were worried that if they mentioned the massive elephant in the room I'd break down there and then.

I found out from a colleague (one I didn't know well) more than a year later that he had had no idea about Andrew's death. He was on holiday at the time and no-one ever mentioned it to him when he returned. So perhaps half the office never knew. In a way that would have made more sense!

But on this first day back my mind was not thinking of rational explanations, and all I felt was an enormous gulf between me and everyone else. I couldn't understand why such a horrendous, nightmarish experience was barely acknowledged.

I scrolled through my very full inbox and opened emails from a couple of Andrew's friends I'd met at the funeral, who had asked to keep in touch. I spent ages reading them, feeling more of a connection with these people I'd talked to for around 15 minutes, than I did with colleagues I'd worked with for two and a half years.

They represented a connection to Andrew of course, the only person I wanted to see. I sat at my desk and stared at my computer and imagined meeting Andrew in town after work, him in his jeans and pink shirt and trainers and glasses and with his toothy smile and saying in his playful accent "Hello Princess" and being reunited and drowning in happiness.

On the work front things improved a little over the next few weeks. Female colleagues asked me how things were when we met in the toilets (never in the actual office) plus I had a great manager and deputy manager. Thoughtful, intelligent people who I could actually talk to; very different to power-hungry, robotic or unhinged superiors I'd had in the past.

I tried to get distracted at work and think merely about the next hour or so; sometimes it worked, a lot of times it didn't. Often I felt stuck, sat there at my computer in a windowless office.

The print journalism industry was in peril, with newspapers making huge losses and frequent redundancies, so lord knows there was a gloomy feeling in the air at the best of times. Now, if a wave of grief hit, the atmosphere felt so sad and seriously claustrophobic.

I scanned death notices for news of other sudden, untimely deaths so I felt connected to something. I'd frequently take a screen break and go for a drink of water, or just to stand in the canteen and look out of the window at a different view. Occasionally I didn't go in at all, if I'd had no sleep or when the whole place – and life – just seemed too alien.

The day after we scattered Andrew's ashes at Musselburgh harbour, one day in January 2011, I returned to work as though I'd been away on everyday business. I couldn't comprehend the idea that Andrew really was gone forever, and so the ashes part seemed like a surreal subplot, too ludicrous to be true.

On the train from Carlisle I'd stared into the distance and concentrated hard. I had a very fond memory of walking round the harbour with Andrew on a summer's night a few months before. Walking, talking, laughing, holding hands, kissing. And now he was simply ashes? Not possible! It was like I was stumped by a crossword clue or mathematical puzzle and what my brain could not grasp I put to one side.

The next day I lost myself in work and afterwards went to the first class in an evening cookery course I'd signed up to, in an effort to continue with life.

Pizza was on this first lesson menu. As I kneaded the dough, images of the harbour, the sea, flowers on the wet sand came into my thoughts. While everyone else's culinary creations came out of the oven looking neat and normal, my base was comically thick and so packed with toppings it started collapsing as I tried to lift it. I took it home and tried a slice. But back in my lonely reality it – and the very act of eating – was so unappealing I may as well have been chewing wet concrete.

During those bleak days I wanted to wear a T-shirt – no *I ♥ Carlisle* this time (that happiness was a world away now) but one declaring I AM RECENTLY BEREAVED. Or even just BEREAVED.

So if I lacked concentration while doing an interview, or was late for a meeting, or was slow filling up at a garage forecourt, then the explanation for not always functioning seamlessly in daily life was there for all to see.

I read about women in Victorian times who followed full mourning for a year, dressed all in black, then in the second year moved into half mourning where they could wear hats and muted colours. What a wonderful idea, and this from an era associated with a suppression of emotions. Why was it that, a century on, grief seemed to be more of a taboo subject than ever?

Outside work I trusted my instinct to find things that would help me move through my grief.

I kept a journal. I met up with people I knew I could talk about Andrew with, so when they asked "How are you?" I felt able to tell them and expand on "up and down" or "okay today". I bought a storage box and placed mementos in it. Some had been given to me by his family, including a photo album. Neither of us liked having our photos taken so I had none of him or of us together.

I had a couple of postcards and notes from Andrew but, mostly, texts. If we had had longer together I'm quite sure there would have been letters too, but our first months of romance were played out using this most modern way of communicating.

My phone deleted texts automatically when the memory got full and ones sent in the early days of our relationship had already gone.

So, panicking that I'd lose the rest, I typed up every text from our last months together. There were hundreds of them, 227 in October alone, up until my last, unanswered text, sent on the afternoon of 28 October.

I copied them just as they were written, with name, date, time and the message. They jumped from silly to deeply romantic, from mundane to mischievous. They meant everything to me and still do.

It was a heartwrenching task, but I cried so much it was cathartic too. And I thought of the end goal: having them forever. After several hours' work I printed them out and placed them in my memory box. Even to this day I look in it only occasionally, but I feel such a contentedness knowing it's there, like a preserved box of delights.

Andrew's brother and sister-in-law very kindly gave me some money to purchase something or do something in his memory. I gave this some thought. A trip somewhere? Too fleeting. A piece of jewellery? Too small and too easy to lose.

I wanted something that would display and reflect our happy time together on a much bigger scale, something unique I could keep for years to come. I decided on a painting and a couple of months later sought out an artist to commission. Cumbria was awash with talented painters who depicted pretty scenes of the lakes and fells but, once I decided how the painting should look, I knew it would require a slightly leftfield mind.

I hopped between parallel universes, going through the motions in the main one: get up, have breakfast, listen vaguely to the radio, jump in the shower (exhausted already from lack of sleep and the grief swirling around my head) and go to work.

On the way I'd entertain memories and questions, replaying on a loop the times Andrew and I had spent together, and could spend together, before being interrupted by thoughts about his death and remembering he was gone.

Then I'd pack these away like a jack-in-a-box and ascend the stairs to my office, my spinning head and the butterflies in my stomach a sign that I was suppressing thoughts.

Inevitably this was impossible to stick to for more than a few hours, not least because of the constant reminders that life without Andrew was empty.

Once, after a rubbish day at work, as I walked back to my flat in the heavy rain, soggy and cold by the time I got through the front door, I remembered a day that previous summer, walking back to my flat in the heavy rain, soggy by the time I got through the front door.

That time, I picked up my post which included a parcel. I recognised the writing and it gave me a buzz. I laughed when I opened it: a quarter pound of white mice, one of my favourite sweets. This time I walked through the door, soggy and cold and, as I saw there was no post, remembered picking up that parcel, feeling that buzz and the laughter. I drew the curtains to shut out the world, got into bed and cried for so long my pillow was soaking wet by the time I fell asleep.

On brighter days I found work a great distraction and was glad to have a daily structure and what could be a varied and interesting job. I mean *really* glad – my raw emotions sporadically making me feel inspired and thankful for everything.

It was the winter of 2010, a proper, freezing winter, the coldest in years. Carlisle was covered in snow for weeks on end. The windows in my flat iced up on the inside and I had my portable heater on almost constantly, conveniently forgetting an alarming utility bill would soon arrive. Outside though it reminded me of a Scandinavian winter, with the constantly crisp air, blue skies and sunshine.

I took a different route to work and felt a real appreciation for life. I lapped up everything before me. Fellow workers walking across the pedestrianised city centre, quiet but for high heels clipping on the ground and strains of conversation floating through the air. Lorries parked outside shops and cafés, the metal shutters half open, men carrying delivery boxes inside. The city starting up for the day.

There was a café open and already bustling; you could hear the clatter of plates and the burr of Cumbrian accents. Who were these people, not just up and out but ready to socialise and laugh at half past eight in the morning? I liked the atmosphere they created.

I'd walk through the cathedral grounds, admiring the timelessly handsome surroundings covered in a blanket of snow. Further on along West Walls, an elevated viewpoint which showed the railway line below, houses and factories beyond. Round the corner and down Castle Way. This was a plainer part of Carlisle, noisy with queues of traffic on the dual carriageway which, on cold, rainy, sad days, seemed ugly.

Now with the icing sugar-white pavements beneath crisp skies, painted blue with a few strokes of pink and wisps of smoke, I thought it looked breathtaking. I felt a connection with Carlisle and could feel the rhythms of life pounding through me.

Those rare, high feelings were quite something. But there were so many bad days too, relentless in their emptiness, when the world lost its colour completely. Things weren't even a stark black and white, just a washed out grey.

Other people felt a million miles away. Snippets of small talk sounded, to my chaotic mind, like nonsense. I watched people's lips move but they may as well have been dubbed into a foreign language.

I felt like the woman in *Brief Encounter*, when a neighbour she meets on the train speaks at her (not to her) and you hear her inner monologue, about how agonizingly lonely she feels. And he, without a clue, carries on talking.

I stopped going out with large groups of friends or to leaving dos, and avoided girly nights in the pub where everyone seemed to stick to a script, as most of us do day to day, circling round the same subjects: relationships, upcoming weddings, what design of kitchen to get, summer holiday destinations.

I was fascinated by our social norms. You would never meet an acquaintance who's expecting a baby or getting married and not ask them how they are and how it's all going. Yet when it's someone who's dealing with the one given in life – death – it's often deemed not worthy of mention, or too tricky to talk about. It seems the script reads:

Happy news: Good! Proceed!
Bad news: Avoid! Repeat: Avoid!

And with many people I met, it was clear the subject of death was not on the agenda at all. Perhaps people assume you won't want to talk about what's happened; that bringing it up will reopen old wounds, or cause some kind of public breakdown.

I understand that it's an awkward subject to broach, especially if you have no experience of bereavement. That many people are worried about not knowing what to say, or saying the wrong thing.

But my reality was a world away from this kind of reasoning. As I had Andrew in my mind every moment of every day for at least the first year after he died, it seemed to me the most obvious topic of conversation at a lunch or on a night out.

And I would always have preferred people to attempt to say something, even if it was admitting they didn't know what to say. So what if it's a bit clunky and doesn't sound like something you would read in a carefully crafted sympathy card?

The point is it reaches out to the bereaved, offering a connection to the human world, a hand to hold, even if only for a few minutes. And that means so much.

The less space I had to talk about my grief, the more I retreated into myself. And I got that people might not always want Queen Victoria in their company, so I stuck to meeting people one-to-one, positive people who were comfortable talking about Andrew and about death.

At the occasional larger social gatherings I attended, on the days when I felt up to it, I (having got the message over those first couple of months) didn't bring up the subject of Andrew.

Sometimes after work I still had such a longing, a yearning, to see Andrew that I'd walk into town and sit on our bench. There, for a few moments, I felt more at one with the world than anywhere else.

In the evening I went running with no route in mind. I enjoyed pounding the pavements, past people's front rooms and kitchens – people living normal lives, which I was a part of by day. But now I speeded up to a pace that suited the thoughts whirring through my head.

One evening I ran up to the park in the pitch black. I headed along a thin ledge of grass at one side of a sports field, about four metres higher than the pitch itself. I couldn't see the surface properly in the darkness and wished I could slip off the edge into oblivion.

It was a clear night and I looked up at the stars and asked Andrew if he was there. "If so, if you can hear me, please make things more bearable!" I pleaded.

Often, towards the end, I'd run to what had been one of our favourite places in Carlisle and stand there, rooted to the spot, reluctant to return to the cold reality.

One week a sadness took hold – which I was used to – but this time it did not ease. I had no desire to go running and wondered if an exercise class would help, if only so the endorphins would give a temporary lift.

I went to the local leisure centre and did a class – I can't remember which one but it involved sit-ups and squats and dumbbells and made my legs and arms seriously hurt the next day.

Under the yellowy light I watched people come in, of different shapes, sizes and ages. I watched wide-eyed and wondered: had anyone here experienced a tragedy? It was impossible to tell. Afterwards I walked home, feeling high on one level but on another as lost as ever.

I put the radio on in my kitchen and started making something to eat. *Three Little Birds* by Bob Marley came on. It sounded like it was playing far, far away, down the end of a tunnel.

But the strains of the tune reached me and I started not singing along but speaking it. There was no joy or lilt in my voice, it was just a monotone chant: "And every little thing… is gonna be alright…"

Yet as I spoke those words I also felt touched by them. I stopped cooking and stood in the middle of my kitchen and lifted my arms out wide and then stretched them up above my head, placing my hands together. I breathed in, drinking up this feeling, which was tinged with a positivity I'd not felt for ages.

Questions, questions. From the deep to the mundane, for those first few months – during the moments I understood he had gone – they spun around my head at such a furious rate I felt dizzy.

Why had Andrew died now? Was there a reason? Did he have any feeling that morning that it was his last? What were his final thoughts? Was he even aware of what was happening? Was it as instant and painless as I'd hoped and prayed? Would he still be here had we not got together – was I a curse? Was it somehow my fault that this most terrible of things had happened? Why were we not given longer together? Why didn't we die together? Would I see him again? Could he see me now? And if he could then was this at all times? On the bog, sleeping, crying? Did he know all my bad habits? Could any good come out of this? Could I ever be happy again? Could I ever be fearless again?

I became convinced I was going to die and went to the doctor to complain of prolonged headaches, chest pains and stiff limbs.

I asked if it was possible to have a series of medical tests on the NHS, to determine just how long I had to live. Did I have heart disease or was a stroke imminent?

The doctor advised that I could go down this route, but even if everything showed up as normal that could change within a year or so. Alternatively, she suggested, I could see a counsellor and talk through my fears and anxieties.

I panicked whenever I couldn't contact people I cared about. When visitors left I asked them to text when they arrived home and could not relax until they did. Unanswered calls to mobiles set my heart racing, taking me right back to the night Andrew died.

The only conclusion was they had died suddenly too and I paced around my house, picturing them in a morgue and imagining what their funeral would be like, until they phoned back and I'd answer with a mixture of glee and relief: "YOU'RE ALIVE!"

SPRING EMPTINESS

Those first few months and the extreme highs and lows were exhausting, but I preferred that clash of emotions to the numb depression that set in.

Like many people I always get a boost from the arrival of spring; a glorious flipside to seemingly never-ending British winters. Every year I'd witness the seasons working to rhythm and feel safe in the knowledge that life is in tune.

Yet there's also a sense of magic. Blooming spring flowers seem to appear overnight, adding patches of colour to dull days or sparkling in the sunshine, nature's palette becoming ever brighter against the backdrop of blue skies. Those first warm days are fabulous, when you can leave your coat at home (so unimaginable just a week earlier), sit in parks filled with people eagerly soaking up the rays, and drink up the fresh feeling of hope that's in the air.

But this spring of 2011 was different. The longer days and sunshine were covered in a grey blanket and I stopped feeling anything at all.

Just as everything staying the same – work, other people's lives, conversations about Christmas and summer holidays – reminded me of what was missing, so too did the new season.

Cumbria is one of the most beautiful places I've ever been to, and my favourite place from which to greet spring. Driving along remote country lanes, past hosts of daffodils (oh yes, they are everywhere), gambolling lambs, working farms, lush greens and shimmering blues as far as the eye can see.

And I'd loved living in Carlisle, which reminded me of a children's book about a typical small English city.

You could flick through the pages and see Bitts Park, with its neat floral displays, rose garden, kids' play park and tennis courts. The cathedral and its pretty grounds (which I always referred to as the churchyard – it seemed a more fitting description of the relaxed space). Carlisle United fans in their blue and white scarves, walking along Warwick Road on Saturdays come rain or shine. The annual Cumberland Show with marmalades, carved walking sticks and children's cupcakes; hundreds of entries taking pride of place in various marquees, a kind of A-Z smorgasbord of creativity and county pride. People buying cuts of meat and cheeses from local farms at the independent butchers and grocers in town, frequently stopping to say hello to friends and neighbours...

And so on. All picture perfect – and now too perfect, too nice, too much a reminder of life, Part 1. There's a succinct quote I really like (by Anais Nin I believe): *We do not see things as they are, we see them as we are.*

I'd been happy and enjoyed the general contentedness of Cumbria. Now the simplicity, the prettiness and the neatness annoyed me. I felt suffocated and stuck in a world which was all wrong. Andrew was no longer here, so what was there to enjoy, appreciate or look forward to?

I drove too fast, walked across roads without looking, shoved junk food down my throat. I truly didn't care if I didn't wake up the next day, and so many times I actively wished I wouldn't. Life had no flavour; it was like existing on a diet of supermarket tomatoes and dry cardboard-like crackers.

I had thought moving through grief was the thing to do, to get through the pain and be able to live a life in the future. But one day, sitting in the churchyard, I felt just as empty as I had wearing my eskimo slippers and huddling under a blanket in my icy flat in midwinter. Nothing had changed in months! No progress.

My heart sank and then I felt angry. I stomped home and threw my grief books across the room, bashing the pages against the wall. Their assurances that there were stages you go through and things slowly got better seemed, at this precise moment in time, like a cruel lie. (Yet a few weeks later, when the depression still had a hold, those same books were the one thing I found I could connect with.)

Some days I craved excitement. So what if it would be short-lived? I wanted something grittier, something stimulating, something to wake me up.

Yet when I tried the odd exciting experience – for example for a feature story I got to experience a quick plane ride over the outskirts of Carlisle – I didn't *feel* it. I looked at the view below and was conscious of being in the air, but it was as though I was watching someone else doing it. I didn't feel excitement or fear, just a heavy nonchalance.

I wondered about moving to another city. But I knew, from reading advice about grief and listening to my own instinct, that moving in the first year after a bereavement is not a good idea. Nothing can magically rid us of grief, no matter where in the world we live.

Still, I longed to be somewhere more suited to my mind and found some solace reading about Mexico's Day of the Dead. Celebrating the lost person, mixing heartache with a joy and a celebration of a life very well lived. What a beautiful idea. *So perfect for you, Andrew*, I thought.

I tried to keep going and continued to go to work, though the office felt more sterile than ever.

After my birthday in March I took in cute cards made by my nieces and nephews and placed them on my desk. They made me think of buds blossoming and I'd avert my eyes from the robotic black text on my computer screen and dream instead about diving into those painted colours, bathing briefly in a pool of happiness.

I still wasn't sleeping but got used to going to work on about four hours. I'd learned back at the beginning not to try to force sleep, nor panic about not getting enough.

I frequently woke in the middle of the night but, with the light now always on, I'd remember my situation immediately. Most times I'd get up, calmly make a cup of tea, take it back to bed and listen to the World Service or Radio 5 live's *Up All Night*. Feeling part of an after-hours community of shift workers, people in different time zones, night owls and insomniacs brought a momentary comfort.

By early spring I had a car – a dinky little Toyota Yaris which was a pleasure to drive and, at first, a much-needed passport to freedom. Now it was just a machine, a convenient cage in which to store my sadness.

Having no interest in the surrounding environment, I stopped walking to work and drove. At lunchtimes I drove to the supermarket. After work I drove out of Carlisle and along country lanes, with no end point in mind.

Sometimes I'd drive up the M6 to a coffee shop at a motorway service station near Gretna. I'd sit in the car park eating a bland toasted sandwich, looking out at the gravelly car park and the muddy fields beyond, then drive back home.

In the early days I'd enjoyed walking as it was a pace which allowed me to be conscious of every breath and sort through the thoughts stacked in my mind, like leafing through a photo album. Sometimes running had been the right pace.

Now I robotically drove around the outskirts of Carlisle in vast circles or zigzagged through west Cumbria, with no destination and no desire for the journey to end. It was a listless limbo in the middle of nowhere but certainly preferable to going home.

I tried a holiday abroad but hated it; all I felt were overwhelming memories of a holiday with the same group a year before, when my romance with Andrew was starting and life was magic. The contrast felt like a waking nightmare.

I couldn't fathom how everything could carry on the same as always – conversation topics, group photos in front of tourist attractions and merry evenings out – when my world was so different now. My friends, being nice people, of course asked me if I was okay. But my sadness was so heavy I felt I was drowning in it, and I couldn't articulate how I was feeling.

Back in Carlisle I still met the odd friend for a coffee at weekends, but I felt so far away from their world, I wasn't able to feel their kindness or let any happiness or hope seep in. And because my confidence (in myself and the world) had gone, I barely knew how to express myself anymore.

I felt lethargic and deeply bored. I was bored of work, bored of culture, bored of nature, bored of Carlisle.

The news annoyed me (mind you I wasn't alone – mind-numbing coverage of the royal wedding was everywhere).

TV programmes, magazine articles and films annoyed me, except ones about tragedy and death. They were few and far between; mostly I seemed to come across perfect couples and perfect families and storylines where people walk into the sunset and live happily ever after.

I stopped reading and watching TV and got addicted to a game on my mobile phone. One where coloured bubbles drop down and you have to match up the colours to erase a line, a little like Tetris. I'd been slightly addicted to Tetris as a teenager, playing it on my dad's BBC computer after nights out clubbing with a friend, hitting replay until we couldn't keep our eyes open, desperate to increase our PB scores.

I had also taken afternoons off school to get to the next stage in Sonic the Hedgehog. Ever the conscientious pupil! But I'd had a life at the same time; it was part of a very full week and mixed in with school, boyfriends, parties and good times. This was something else! It was an instant, always accessible means of escape and I was hooked. I played it until the early hours of the morning, during my lunch break in my car, as soon as I got back from work and well into the evening. It brought no happiness or change but mirrored my zombie existence. The perfect fit.

When I looked at my situation objectively over those months it was clear my depression was a completely natural response to what had happened.

When someone you love dies suddenly and YOU WILL NEVER SEE THEM AGAIN how could you *not* feel depressed?

The worst thing was that I knew if I was depressed because of a job or a relationship that wasn't working out, I would do something about it. I had in the past. But I could not change this and it was like slamming my head against a brick wall. I COULD NOT CHANGE THIS.

I got scared. What if I never came out of it? I could not see any reason to continue with life if this was how it was going to be from now on.

Yet I must have had one, somewhere, because the day came when I asked for help. I made an appointment at my surgery and, when it came, felt nervous about going in and announcing I needed support. Even after all that had happened it felt like a big step.

I saw a doctor I'd never seen (my surgery had a pool of doctors and you saw whoever was available). He was a lovely man with a soft voice and gentle manner. He listened to what I said, took off his glasses, rubbed his eyes with his index finger and thumb and sighed deeply.

He looked very sad and said: "You know, I am very sorry for you, for this to happen at your age. You should be older, in your 70s or 80s, when at least you and your companion have been together for a long time and you will know other people in the same situation.

"You will get through this. Depression is natural because your life as you know it has ended. But new threads will come in, in time, and you will live a new life and enjoy it. I am sure of that."

Those words wrapped themselves around me like a hug.

He arranged an appointment with the surgery counsellor – at least, it said counsellor on the sign on her door. What I encountered was a woman who couldn't have had less empathy or interest in other people. She obviously hadn't read the notes about why I was there and, when filling in a form with my details, asked about my partner. I looked at her in amazement.

"Ah, so EX partner – that's why a lot of people come here!"

"Er, no, he's not an ex, he died last year."

Sitting draped in a pashmina and jangling her chunky bangles, she talked about her own experience of death, pausing every so often and staring at me through her thick glasses for what seemed like an eternity.

I recorded a couple of nuggets in my journal:

Me: "I'm here because, while friends and family are supportive, I feel like I now need someone else to talk to."

Her: "I'm not surprised. After all, your friends will just be thinking, 'Thank god this hasn't happened to me.'"

Me: "I've found the lack of acknowledgement difficult to deal with; lots of people never mention Andrew's death, ask about who he was, or how I am coping with it all."

Her: "It's better people say nothing than saying the most stupid things."

Me: "I'd rather people say something, I don't care if it's not the perfect thing."

Her: "Well you obviously haven't had people say stupid things to you then."

Her: "Well, it's a unique experience. And it's SHIT. You don't get better, you just get used to it."

Me: "Um, it can be shit, but that's why I wanted to see someone, in the hope it will help me feel better and able to live life again."

I walked home in a daze, incredulous that this woman was being paid to give vulnerable people advice.

I looked elsewhere. I had heard of the bereavement charity Cruse, found the local branch online and sent a message. They emailed back the next day and I later spoke to the loveliest woman on the phone, who acknowledged my loss, was sympathetic and gave me an assurance I would see a counsellor soon.

She said there was a waiting list but, once you started seeing someone, there was no time limit. You kept seeing them until it felt right to stop.

This information filled me with delight. I'd always known, deep down, that grief could not be rushed, nor expected to end neatly after, say, one year – and that instinct was being validated by a charity dealing with bereavement.

They posted me a booklet, entitled *After the death of*

someone very close, and I read it from cover to cover. With its gentle, understanding and positive tone, it became one of my most treasured possessions and still makes me cry to this day.

My counsellor from Cruse was a gentle, kind woman who had lost her husband at quite a young age – so I knew she would understand. When I arrived for our meeting, in a non-descript room above a church, she said: "This is your time."

We met regularly for just over a year and it proved to be a lifeline. Her and my homeopath Beth's nurturing consultations were invaluable, keeping me going through some dark, dark days.

SUMMER HOPE

I had been avoiding Edinburgh, now a location connected with such sadness. But in late May I decided to go for a weekend, to try it out.

I visited Musselburgh harbour, where we had scattered Andrew's ashes, with my twin sister and Lucy, the gangly greyhound who slid about the back seat of my wee Yaris like she was on the waltzers.

We ate memorial sweets and chatted and walked along the beach and had a lovely afternoon. That evening I went out for a pizza with my mum and we wandered around the centre of Edinburgh in sunshine and showers.

And a funny thing happened. I had been expecting to feel awful, to be paralysed by sadness and hate being there. Instead, as we strolled through the handsome streets I didn't just think of memories of Andrew. They were mixed in with other memories, many others. I remembered that before this all happened I was someone! I had an identity, a personality, a spirit. If I had a life before, could I have one again?

Thanks to fortnightly meetings with my Cruse counsellor, visits from various friends and family, the arrival of my painting, longer lighter days and a new-found strength to appreciate them, I felt more positive when summer came.

When my sisters visited, in late June, it felt symbolic as the last time they were down, in November, I was deep in shock. I couldn't have imagined having a good time ever again. We went out for dinner and I suggested we order a bottle of sparkling wine to celebrate getting through the last few months. It wasn't that everything was fine, but that it felt right marking that progress. And after months of trauma and feeling battered and bruised, it felt good to be kind to myself.

I joined a dance class and loved it. Pure escapism and great exercise too. That hour every Tuesday was the one time I didn't think about Andrew.

My thoughts seemed to flow more, and one day I had a mini-epiphany: I decided not to worry about not accepting Andrew had gone. *I can't accept it, so I can't accept it.* This simple yet powerful realisation made me feel more at peace and everything seemed more fluid.

I went to a wedding in a Cumbrian village and had a ball. The groom even mentioned Andrew in his speech, along with other people who had passed away and who had been special to guests. People who should have been there with us. It was so thoughtful and so touching and also echoed exactly what I'd thought when I got up that morning. That acknowledgement, stated in just a few words, freed my thoughts so I could get in the moment more, and everything suddenly felt looser and lighter.

The other guests I knew were good company and I didn't feel lonely. We drank homemade elderflower wine, watched sword dancers and ceilidh danced. We laughed and sang stupid songs and in the middle of the night trudged back through the mud to our tents, and I had the best sleep I'd had for ages (due in no small part to the elderflower concoction I'm sure).

I even tried a hen weekend which involved canoeing on Lake Windermere – what fun that was – but headed home that night, avoiding the girly evening with the stripper. My idea of a nightmare, whether bereaved or not.

On a family holiday in Dumfries and Galloway I felt a surge of gratefulness that everyone was alive and well, especially my mum, who had been diagnosed with cancer a few years earlier. She enjoyed these holidays and was in good spirits this summer.

Our handsome holiday house was straight out of an Enid Blyton novel, my nieces and nephews made me laugh and I had a new found energy and a desire to get out and about.

We went mountain biking and played badminton and, as it was such good weather, even sunbathed at the beach and swam in the sea. Wigtown's charming, old-school summer festival was on and we attended the pet show in the car park, played bingo in the town hall and had cream teas in the bowling clubhouse. On the warm, dry evenings we sat out in the garden, slathering on the midgie repellent, chatting and watching bats flying through the clear night sky and rooks nesting in the trees.

I made the most of the fun times. Not only had they been a long time coming but I often felt them much more than I would have before Andrew died, something eloquently described by my old friend Kahil Gibran: *The deeper sorrow carves into your being, the more joy you can contain.*

And these times were still few and far between, so they had a kind of novelty value attached to them. In between there was an emptiness, a sadness, a feeling that something was missing. It was relentless, that emptiness, but I hoped it would lift slightly, once a year passed and all the milestones were out the way.

DECISION TIME

I've long been fascinated by our obsession with time. Obeying the clock ticking steadily, day and night, over the Western world. It rules our lives on almost every level, dictating to us when we work, eat, meet friends, relax, and sleep.

People boast about being early birds, of waking naturally at 6am, of cramming so much into one day. That is seen as virtuous and worthwhile.

Those of us who enjoy long lies and occasionally having days with no plans are often viewed more negatively; seen as lackadaisical and aimless and wasting precious time.

In this age, of phones and laptops and the world at your fingertips, to just *be* somewhere – in a café or sitting on a park bench – is so unusual it stands out as strange behaviour.

And so it is with grief. I had arrived here unexpectedly against a backdrop of British society's stiff mores, where the subject is rarely talked about.

And even though I'd seen a bit of the world and become, as an adult, my own person and in touch with my emotions, my Edinburgh upbringing was still an intrinsic part of me. (I always think the stiff, redoubtable Miss Jean Brodie is a brilliant illustration of this Auld Reekie way.)

Therefore I sometimes felt as though I should be progressing through it at a certain rate, that after one year it should definitely be easier. Onwards and upwards.

That work should be an entirely helpful distraction and I should, soon enough, get over it or at the very least get used to it. In our increasingly frenetic society, where you are expected to be doing stuff 24/7, to simply be with my grief beyond the initial raw period felt self-absorbed and indulgent.

Certainly I knew I didn't want to be a victim of this tragic turn of events and let it define me forever more. And many times, in the throes of grief, in the deep centre of that black lagoon, I had longed for time to speed up and transport me to an easier, more peaceful place.

However, I knew in my heart this journey could not be rushed, and continued to see that first year out at its own pace.

But my god it was hard work. As the anniversary approached there were, of course, other milestone dates too; vivid memories that took me right back to loved-up summer weekends and excursions Andrew and I had enjoyed together.

Two days before the anniversary I drove to a village in west Cumbria to do an interview for a feature. This was the last day of work as I'd taken the next three days off.

While sitting listening to the interviewee and taking notes, I suddenly had a kind of otherworldly sensation. The room started going blurry and I felt dizzy. I had to concentrate on looking at her to stop the room from spinning. Was I going to pass out? And then what? Was my time up? 'Tis the season to die, after all.

I couldn't say anything – it would have opened the floodgates and I knew having a meltdown wasn't part of the job – but the interview was soon up, thankfully, and I was so pleased when I stepped outside.

Driving back, the road ahead (a rural road with bends and brows, speed limit 60mph) started going out of focus and I became so aware of the fact I was driving, I started doing so erratically.

I was fixated on each car that passed from the opposite direction – that every few seconds each of us was inches from death or serious injury – and felt terrified that I wouldn't make it back to Carlisle.

I pulled into a lay-by and sat there, my heart pounding as I stared into the distance. After a few minutes I drove back and felt a massive relief entering Carlisle and passing the 30mph sign. Back at the office, still shaking, I told my boss I had to go home and rushed back to my flat and lay down for the whole afternoon, terrified of the outdoor world and too frightened to do anything.

That night I lay in bed and had so many thoughts stored in my mind I thought it was going to explode. When I lay my head on the pillow it felt like it was continuing to fall, making my stomach lurch.

But as I lay there I thought *I have a choice*. I could get on and go with the ride, or rail against it and hate and fear every moment.

So at around 2am I got out of bed. I put some music on and turned the volume up. I loosened up a little and stood in my living room. It had been a while since I'd been swept down into the abyss and I'd been avoiding going back, but now it was time.

Ok grief, come and take me. Take me with you. And my mind took me on a voyage. In the harsh light of reality I was in my cold, quite bare flat, having lost a new lover and treasured friend.

But as I entered this new mind state the flat became bathed in a strange, hazy light and furniture and objects had sharper outlines. I could feel the vibrations of the music and I could see the wallpaper bouncing up and down and the stripes on the sofa moving.

I felt like I was being buoyed up and down, the threadbare blue carpet turning into water. Suddenly I was riding the crest of a wave. The painting was the mast of my ship and I headed forwards. I stood tall and breathed deeply, and imagined myself as a warrior heading to unchartered lands.

For those few minutes I felt strong and lucid, and excited by the thought that fear could become excitement; sadness and tears a catharsis.

And as I went with these feelings I felt lighter; giddy yet relaxed, like I was stoned. I enjoyed my new mind-freedom, going with the moment instead of trying to run away from it, and I slept well that night.

The next day was Andrew's birthday. I'd been dreading it, yet felt filled with contentment as I remembered how happy he was this time last year.

I lay in bed and let the memories dance around my mind...we'd spoken for ages on the phone, early evening and late evening; happy, tender, flirtatious words exchanged. I'd sent him a box of ice cream-shaped cakes and a card, and later he'd sent me a photo of one of the cakes with a candle in it, and I'd wished him a happy, happy, happy birthday.

We could not wait to see each other in two days' time and spoke of plans for the following year. Fun, dreamy plans like going in a hot air balloon across the South

Downs and more real ones, like going to New York for my birthday.

I can feel the pleasure of that evening still, to this day. We were in different cities yet our connection was strong, it was natural, it was joyful.

For the rest of the day I mooched around, doing whatever my instinct suggested, and ended up sitting in the churchyard in the rain eating a celebratory slice of cake. "Happy birthday sweetheart," I whispered to Andrew. "I miss you so, so much, but I'll always be glad your final days were rich and happy."

After the anniversary I had hoped, hoped, hoped things would get easier. In the days after I felt a slight weight had lifted, and a relief I'd got through the year without either dying or having a breakdown, as those two things had seemed so close.

I continued to go to work, to see friends, to visit family in Edinburgh. I don't really remember details, as it was all a bit of a non-time. I was existing, yes, and 'getting used to' life without Andrew. God, how I detest that phrase.

But I gave it a go and tried everything. I made sure I had space to think, to cry, to reflect. I went to work and tried to get lost in writing features and interviewing people with weird and wonderful stories.

I continued to meet with my counsellor from Cruse. I made an effort to socialise but only really one to one; large groups I had very little to say to. I went to my dance class, took up running again, and even moved house.

One day, in early January 2012, I was walking down

the elegant Victorian street to my new flat. It was a clear night, I was living an easy Carlisle life and I thought: *I have everything I need here.* And for a few days I believed I was happy again. And perhaps, temporarily, I was.

One weekend I met a friend for a coffee and told her about my flat – how lovely it was, all the mod cons it had. "There's a dishwasher," I said, smiling half-heartedly. And I felt an emptiness returning.

Then I came down with a chest infection. It was a miserable couple of weeks and, with no-one around to make me a cup of tea or bring me medicine or even just hold my hand and tell me I'd get well soon, extremely lonely.

When I returned to work, during the dark month of February, I felt totally exhausted. I'd go into work robotically, with little interest in stories I was writing.

I'd make myself go for a walk at lunchtime and play songs like *Learning to Fly* by Tom Petty on my MP3 player, the soaring, anthemic tune like a shot of adrenaline to rescue me from this trance-like life. In the evening I'd get home, shut the door and lie on the sofa watching telly.

As the weeks passed I realised this could not go on. I was devastated that life felt the same as the first spring after Andrew died. I was numb, exhausted, defeated. Had I really come through this insane experience to end up like *this?* Sure, I lived in a smart flat (with dishwasher) but I was sleepwalking through life, neither happy nor sad.

I knew Andrew wouldn't have wanted me to end up like this, and I knew deep down I sure as hell didn't want to either. It was clear I had to go somewhere else, but where?

The next day, for the first time in ages, I felt an inner strength. My instinct started working again, and I listened. It was telling me to go. Go and live!

I had no ties. I *had* loved my job but the enjoyment had long gone. I had no children, no mortgage and a pension so paltry I wasn't sure why I was paying into it each month.

Whether I'd even live to retirement age was not certain at all; I could die tomorrow, who could say? All in all, it was clear I had to take this opportunity (one not available to everyone my age) while I was fit and well. And it was the best tribute to Andrew I could think of.

But where to go? I considered somewhere exotic and relaxing – chilling out on a beach somewhere in Thailand perhaps – but knew I needed a purpose. I'd travelled in my 20s and remembered it can soon feel a little aimless.

I daydreamed about going to a garden retreat of some kind and pictured balmy days and floral scents, a kind of healing through nature.

I whetted my appetite with vague internet searches. One day I stumbled across WWOOF, the Worldwide Organisation for Organic Farms. It drew me in and the philosophy struck a chord: exchange work for board and food.

The simplicity held a great appeal. For the first time in so long I felt excited. I knew I had to do it but where? A couple of friends joked about sticking a pin in a map of the world to choose the location.

I thought about my desires and pictured: an abundance of produce. Warm, sociable people who wear their hearts on their sleeves and would be happy to talk about death as well as life. Strong communities with people who look out for one another. Delicious food and wine. Sunshine.

And so it came to me. Italy. It had to be Italy! A well-trodden path by many a person looking to find themselves – but with all the reasons above and more, why wouldn't it be?! And as soon as I thought of it I knew, in the pit of my stomach, it was without a doubt the right move.

I suddenly had a surplus of energy and spent my time organising my trip and working out ways to save money. I arranged to leave my flat and stay with friends, who kindly put me up for a couple of weeks at a time, and sold all my furniture. I planned a very tight budget, cancelling direct debits and stocking up on food at Morrisons (I always went after 8pm, when they started reducing items to bargain prices) and freezing it for the week. I sold most of my possessions at various car boot sales, which was pretty liberating and fun too, thanks to the warm Cumbrian banter.

I booked my train tickets and arranged stays with families in Italy. My only plan was to travel from north to south and I had only these requirements: varied produce and tasks, and that the hosts spoke a little English and sounded like good people.

I kept daydreaming about my new life; feeling free, being productive, eating well and meeting interesting people. In my mind I was already there, and it was a struggle to get out of bed and to the office. I couldn't have had less interest, and can barely remember what I wrote about in those last couple of months.

I was even late for my leaving presentation, as I'd been on the phone to the guy who owned the B&B I'd booked in Turin, my first destination. He had chatted for ages and, with his lovely Italian accent, I had been happy to listen.

My leaving do was a picnic in Bitts Park (one of my favourite Carlisle places) on a beautiful, sunny summer's evening, and included a practice run of putting up the tent I was borrowing from friends.

August soon arrived. I stayed with friends in London and from there, took the Eurostar to Paris then the train to Turin.

I didn't feel anxious at all. Grief had pared everything back, in a spiritual sense, and physically I had no job, no home and no possessions apart from my backpack. I felt an enormous sense of freedom; and light, loose, ready to go. Ready for anything.

I hoped the first place would be good but felt pretty easy-going about it all. If it wasn't, I would just move onto the next farm. This was an open book.

I hadn't read any guides to the areas I'd arranged to stay in. I hadn't even learned any Italian. On the bus to the first farm I had to look in my phrasebook to find out how to say "Pleased to meet you".

Looking back this ignorance was absurd, but it was necessary. This was Part 2 of my life after all; new and unknown. To have predicted or dreamed or hoped for anything just didn't feel right. In many ways I had been born again. I was like a blank canvas in the middle of a studio, ready to be splattered with paint, patterns and pictures forming. And, despite everything that had gone before, there was no doubting this was an exciting and special place to be.

PART 2

…be patient toward all that is unsolved in your heart and try to love the questions themselves, like locked rooms and like books that are written in a very foreign tongue. Do not now seek the answers, which cannot be given you because you would not be able to live them. And the point is, to live everything. Live the questions now.

Rainer Maria Rilke

PIEDMONT

In Turin I remember hailstones crashing down, getting lost, having to check with a local how the subway tickets worked and buying blister plasters (always happens), wandering around in the sun, admiring the baroque architecture, and chilling in my B&B, which I had all to myself.

There was an out of season feel, as this was the month Italians left hot, humid cities in droves and headed to the coast for a few weeks' holiday.

Turin was a welcome change of scene but it was all the experience of a tourist. The jigsaw didn't slot into place until the next night, when I arrived at a little village in south Piedmont. Alessandro, the owner of the farm (called an *orto*), picked me up at the station in his red van, coloured beehives roughly stacked in the back. The faint aroma of honey filled the air and the horizon was dotted with green mountains under piercing blue skies.

Alessandro was tall and thin and had a warm, quiet demeanour. He told me about the area as we drove along, stopping first for a quick look at the *orto*.

Called *Poc Ma Bun*, which translates as small but good, he had started it five years before. Though it was a small area there was lots of produce, including tomatoes, spinach, potatoes, runner beans, onions, lettuce, cabbage, courgettes, raspberries, strawberries, herbs and honey. The produce was sold direct from here, supplied to local restaurants and – as I would happily experience – used for the family meals.

We drove the short distance to the village, past the little school, the church and sunflowers swaying in the breeze. Up a steep winding road, and past a sign that said *privato*, we arrived at his family home; a huge country house at the end of the village.

I opened the car door to be greeted by two of the friendliest dogs, Gringo and Trifola. And then by the mum and dad, Rosa Maria (known as Rosa) and Mario, who were also excited by my arrival – I was their first ever WWOOF volunteer.

The family showed me to my room. It was like a cabin on a ship, with a wooden balcony outside overlooking the village and the mountains. The view was spectacular. There was no eerie country silence (well it can be eerie to this city girl) – nearby the river rushed down from the mountains and at night you could hear the *grilli* (crickets) in the air.

It was soon dinner time. I sat at the table and my new life, Mark 2, began.

Meals were always cooked by Rosa, and always delicious. They told me the names of the dishes in Italian, translated by Alessandro. There were red peppers in olive oil, bread, chick pea fritters, fish, red wine, a cheese board and grappa. I thought I was in heaven!

Mealtimes here were not a case of simply going through the motions, of consuming food as fuel. They were a celebration of all that's good in life: flavour, creativity, conversation and pleasure. And after a lifetime of people commenting on my big appetite (imagine that, a woman consuming more than a salad, *how* un-ladylike!) here it was expected that everyone would participate fully in this most enjoyable of rituals.

Trifola and Gringo settled in under the table and nestled against my feet, so it was like wearing a pair of toasty slippers.

The atmosphere was so welcoming, so convivial, I remember feeling like I was in a dream. Yet unlike at social situations during the past year and ten months, I was very much present.

Neighbours arrived, to see the new guest no doubt, but I discovered they called in most nights anyway. One of them was placid and quiet, and sat smiling and fidgeting with her hands. The other was a petite, tough woman, her grey hair tied in a bun, who smoked cigarettes and only ever accepted an espresso, at the end of the meal.

She talked (or rather shouted) endlessly about things I didn't understand, regularly peppered with exclamations of "Madonna!" and "Mamma mia!". She occasionally barked questions at me, which Alessandro tried to translate.

I loved the way that out of the choice of rooms to socialise in they always chose the kitchen. This is where life happens in Italy.

The next morning my door flew open and Trifola bounded in to say hello, her tail wagging furiously against the bed. And when I remembered where I was, I felt so pleased. It was the first time in so long I'd actually wanted to get up and make the most of the day.

I went through to the kitchen. An espresso maker was heating on the stove and freshly baked bread, homemade jam and biscotti sat on the table, and I was greeted with a chorus of "Buongiorno! Tutto bene?" from Rosa and Mario. I was slightly taken aback. They were so warm and friendly, and it was so different to mornings up until the week before.

Alessandro started at the *orto* very early and had said, when we'd discussed start times, he believed it is best when people work to their own rhythms.

So I headed down after breakfast with Mario in his little Fiat Panda, Trifola in the back. Mario had a gentle but outgoing manner. He was sparky and funny and, at 74, he was amazingly active.

His poor eyesight meant he was no longer allowed on the main roads, only these rural ones. But he seemed to know by instinct as much as sight where to slow down, and where to creep round potholes and bumps in the road.

It was a sunny morning and as we drove along I couldn't believe this was work as I knew it now. In fact it was only for a little over three weeks but this didn't enter my mind. Because for the first time in so long I was in the moment and I felt happy.

Workwise that first morning we picked *zucchine* (courgettes). Mario spoke no English and I spoke no Italian, though of course we understood numbers and instructions so long as they were accompanied by actions.

And yet, despite our language barrier, we got on like a house on fire. Many times his actions or expressions would make me laugh loads, and vice versa.

While the family could have seen me as stupid or lazy for not speaking Italian, they really just took me for who I was. To me it said a lot about their kind hearts and gentle spirits.

At mealtimes Alessandro (and older brother Marco, who stayed some weekends) did a great job of translating, sometimes aided by his Italian-English dictionary, which we came to refer to as The Bible. And I carried an Italian dictionary and phrasebook everywhere; to the *orto*, on daytrips, and even just to the kitchen table.

Rosa was so hospitable, always making sure I was okay. Checking I had enough food on my plate at dinner times, that I'd had a good sleep, if my working day had been fine.

Once a week she insisted on doing my washing for me. I'd return after work and find my clothes on the bed, in the neatest pile I'd ever seen, my knickers so intricately folded they looked like a form of origami.

One lunchtime Mario asked me how I'd travelled to Italy and when I told him about the Eurostar going through the Channel Tunnel, he asked if you got to view sea life while travelling through it.

When I explained (translated by Marco) that you didn't see anything, that it was a black tunnel, his disappointment was palpable. He could barely believe the opportunity to ride through water hadn't been turned into a sea life wonderland, Steve Zissou-style. This is how he saw the world.

Alessandro's girlfriend Mara was also staying and working at the *orto*. She was petite, wiry and very fit. She was always doing something – harvesting in the fields or making pesto or *dolce salame* (a chocolate and nut dessert rolled into a sausage shape) in the kitchen.

Many mornings she would ride away on her bike, to go swimming or cycle through the mountains, and appear at some point later, always moving around at whirlwind speed.

In the kitchen at night there was the aroma of freshly cut herbs or baked bread, mixed in with the scent of freshly shampooed hair (they always showered at night rather than in the morning).

Mara laughed a lot and spoke only a little English. Typical of this place, it didn't really matter. In the fields, where we were harvesting potatoes, she would use the hoe and hack away at the dry earth. Then we would both dig away to find the potatoes. (We had the smaller variety one night for dinner, hot with butter and gorgonzola. Delicious!)

Each time, as she started to use the hoe, she would announce: "*Attenzione*! Your hands!" and then we'd dig deep in the soil like two kids playing.

The first few days I was there she would ask if everything was okay and say: "You need something, I am *down*," really emphasising the down and pointing downstairs to her bedroom. On sunny mornings she'd exclaim about the "Blue, blue, BLUE sky!" while looking out of the window at the beautiful view.

I liked talking to her and laughing with her and, again, despite the language barrier (or proving there's much more to a bond than just words), I felt a connection with her.

Late one afternoon we were standing on the shaded terrace of the house weighing herbs, which would be bagged and sold at markets at the weekend. I told her about my situation, about Andrew and how I had come to be here.

"I am sorry," she said slowly, looking genuinely concerned. She patted her chest and added, "That is very hard for your heart."

She asked if I had come to Italy to forget everything, to leave it all behind and I said yes, in a way; I at least wanted to live life again. But I was also here because I had experienced, in the most brutal way, that we don't know what's around the corner. She nodded. "We have one life! Only one!" she declared.

Before we left for the potato field she grabbed me and gave me a tight hug and a warm smile.

As it would turn out, in each place I stayed I met one person I felt comfortable talking to about Andrew (two at a farm in Tuscany, a lovely English-Italian couple who were happy chatting about the meaning of life).

A confidante would always be there, as if by magic. With some people I told them about it briefly, with others more in-depth. However the conversation happened, it always felt right acknowledging why I was in Italy, while not wallowing in the terrible experience with every single person I met.

These were hot, sunny days in Piedmont and nature was all around. While the work itself could have been monotonous – picking tomatoes, peas, runner beans; cleaning onions; digging up potatoes – it wasn't. There was a rhythm to it I liked. I really enjoyed using my body to work; stretching and using muscles, not sat slumped at a computer.

I loved how it was not about being the fastest or the strongest. So much of life is about the end goal, and how to get there ahead of the pack. For many people it is one long competition. So much so we exhaust ourselves so that we don't have the energy to appreciate our achievement, or are too busy already moving onto the next race.

Here, because I was under no pressure at all, I had loads of positive energy to spend. I didn't worry about being too slow or making mistakes. I worked more naturally and, therefore, far more efficiently.

And working outdoors and feeling the sun was wonderful. I watched Trifola run around chasing bees and studied huge spiders weaving webs on the tomato plants. I could hear insects buzzing in the air; that still, warm summer air which makes days seem endless.

At night – and this happened at almost every farm – I flopped into bed exhausted, happy in the knowledge I would be asleep in minutes and slumber so deeply I'd wake feeling totally revived.

People who came to buy produce were so friendly, always stopping to chat. They asked why I had come to Italy. I said I wanted to live life and enjoy a change of scene and, quite often, they'd ask whether my decision was connected to the Mayan calendar and the supposed end of the world on 21 December 2012.

The young daughter of a neighbour would arrive with her grandfather, who was the local grappa maker. She was a beautiful little girl with a shy smile, big eyes and a cartoon-ish bob, and she would always bring me a bunch of flowers picked from her garden. I loved hearing her accented "Ciao Rose-a-line!" as they approached, then her grandfather's animated "Buongiorno! Come stai?!"

The local, slightly eccentric farmer would ride past in his tractor and every few days herd his cattle to the next field, huffing and puffing and shouting. The first time I witnessed it from up the road, before the first cows came into view, I thought he was having some kind of meltdown.

One day, while we were sitting outside the shed cleaning onions, Mario put on a cassette and started singing along – "*La luna Mexicaaana...*" – in an over-the-top, crooner style, making me laugh as usual.

There was a guy helping at the *orto*, through a kind of care in the community programme in the area. We always said a cordial good morning to each other, nothing more, but one day we both got a fit of giggles when I lost grip of the hose I was using to wash crates of potatoes and it soaked us with water.

These fun times and working at the back of the orto, sorting potatoes into sizes and cleaning onions, made me feel like a kid again, and I remembered picnics in the Meadows in Edinburgh or in our back garden. Sunny summer days with bread, Babybels, fruit and juice, and not a worry in the world.

Even the counting and vocabulary-building felt like it was from a kid's viewpoint. Now, when I say or hear words like *cucchiaino* (teaspoon), *macchina* (car), *lampone* (raspberry) or *borsa* (bag), I am taken back to that time in Piedmont.

I'd taken to walking to the *orto* each day rather than get a lift with Mario, to savour every sight, sound and happy feeling. At first I listened to my MP3 player out of habit but soon stopped: I didn't need a boost from the likes of Tom Petty.

And oh how alive I felt. The scuttling of lizards, the ringing of church bells, streams running downhill: all of these sounds almost took on a power of their own and I had a full awareness of everything around me.

I saw and heard completely new things, like wildflowers that looked like balls of cotton wool and the sound of marmosets on a trip to Ceresole Reale.

Pranzo (lunch) was a major part of the day and always took place at *mezzogiorno* (midday). Alessandro and I joked that *mezzogiorno* was like Cinderella's midnight; we simply had to get back to the house in time.

No-one dared be late and when we walked back through the streets they were deserted, such was the importance of lunch.

Mario, like most people his age, had his routines and it was, according to him, imperative we stop work before 12 for lunch and before 8, for dinner. This suited me; by noon I was always hungry and at lunchtime the temperature had crept up to around 32 degrees.

Back at the house we'd watch a TV programme, an afternoon drama about a seal who saved people's lives – every time. We'd all watch it quite intently before tucking into our delicious lunch, the news on in the background.

After lunch we had a siesta or relaxed on the terrace

and chatted, then returned to work around 4pm until *cena* (dinner time).

One lunchtime Alessandro and Mara had to go and do some urgent errands. I had lunch with Mario and Rosa and despite our language barrier we conversed anyway, with words getting lost in translation and stories becoming wildly mixed up.

It reminded me of Mr Forgetful in the *Mr Men* series (the message he's meant to relay, "There's a sheep loose in the lane" turns into a panicky "There's a goose asleep in the rain!") and the surreal world we'd accidentally constructed was so funny we all ended up in hysterics.

Even the steely neighbour who'd called in was chuckling hard by the end, regularly interspersed with "MADONNA!" which made me laugh even more.

One weekday there was no work – it was *Ferragosto*, a national holiday. There was a buzz in the air as the wooden table and chairs outdoors were swept down, the barbecue started, the table set.

And then we had what I can only describe as a feast. Steaks cooked on the barbecue by Mario; and bread, pasta, apple and chocolate cake with a spoonful of raspberry jam, all homemade in the kitchen by the industrious Rosa and Mara.

The courses just kept on coming and the wine and conversation flowed, in tune to other families' chat and song coming from back gardens around the village. I cannot think of a better way to spend an afternoon.

During my stay I had spent all my time at the top of the house. This was the entrance from where the cars were parked, and where my bedroom, the bathroom and the kitchen were.

Over lunch one day they spoke about Mario's collection of things, and joked about his museum in the downstairs rooms. I asked if I could visit, where I could buy a ticket. "For you, it's free," he said, laughing.

The next day, after lunch, Mario and Marco took me to see two rooms at the bottom of the house.

It was like entering a treasure trove. There were intricate wood carvings, comic collections, toy cars from when Marco and Alessandro had been young. Stamp collections, neatly filed, country by country. Tins and cigarette cases. Butterflies in cabinets, the rainbow colours glistening away.

Unsurprisingly Mario showed everything off very proudly; years of care and attention had gone into this collection of gems.

At the end, as we stood at the doorway, he surveyed the room and said softly (translated by Marco): "They are only small things, but they are important to me. They are precious."

TUSCANY AND UMBRIA

My next stay was in Tuscany and the view changed as the train travelled south. The colours turned into muted oranges and reds, and much of the landscape was parched after weeks with no rain. I already missed the vibrant green of Piedmont and my safe, happy, cartoon life there.

Now that I was in my own company for a while for the first time in weeks, I thought of Andrew and how I had come to be here.

The year before, in 2011, my mind had been filled with memories of our romantic summer in 2010. It was achingly painful; they were such happy, magical days yet there would never be any more. How could that be? Now, in 2012, as well as the memories of our time together, I had memories of those thoughts, after Andrew's death.

So, I wondered, perhaps the brutal, agonising heartache becomes watered down as each year passes? Is that how people start living again; their minds re-wire and in time new thoughts, experiences and feelings filter through?

One thing I was sure of: this travelling life was the perfect place for my current state of mind. And as I stepped off the train I felt a flurry of excitement again. More new horizons.

The owner of the next farm, Fabio, was in his late 40s, tall and muscly with prominent features. Driving back from the station we nearly crashed several times. Partly because he was so busy talking and gesticulating, his hands were hardly ever on the steering wheel; partly because his little dog Pirro was running around at his feet. Pirro barked excitedly and whenever he met someone he would stand on his hind legs and jump for ages, his paws clawing the air, like he was auditioning for a circus.

"Don't drive like this," Fabio announced, before launching into talk about the material world being the scourge of Western society, and how it would all be worth nothing when 21 December came.

He was a man of the world, having worked in cities across Europe and in New York, where he learnt English on the streets. He had started his *orto* in the last few years because, he said: "In the future money will mean nothing. What you need is the ability to grow food."

I stayed at his mum and dad's house, a couple of miles from where he lived. It had been the family home, but the children had moved out long ago and it had a slight emptiness to it. As I sat in my spotless double bedroom it felt more like a hotel.

I ate with the mum and dad and sometimes we were joined by Fabio. As in Piedmont, the food was delicious – homemade pastas and breads, local meats and cheeses, and cake – and meals were nearly always served with home-produced wine. The heat was stifling, around 34 degrees, with no breeze at all, so mealtimes would be fairly quick then we'd all go for a siesta.

The father took me shopping and to run errands with him. One day in the car he was chatting to me – in Italian but by now I understood a little. I could make out: "Don't return to Scotland! Telephone your mother and tell her you will stay here and be with Fabio!"

I tried to explain that not only was I not romantically interested in Fabio, but I had a new, exciting life ahead of me. My trip did not – could not – stop here in Tuscany.

He fixed a bike in his garage so I could use it, and followed me in his car as I cycled to the village. Once I got onto the main road I remembered my instinct for left and right is a bit dodgy at the best of times – now it was all topsy-turvy and there were also two roundabouts on the route. Uh-oh.

I made it to the village centre and stopped in the car park of the supermarket. The dad appeared, throwing his hands in the air and ranting and raving. This was the day I learnt that left in Italian is *sinistra*, and right is *destra*, as he kept drilling into me on the way back to the house, my bike in the boot of his car. The next time I went out, he insisted we have a practice run on the side streets first.

It was true, it had been erratic cycling. But many times in Italy I had a kind of kamikaze attitude. I'd faced the reality of death in Carlisle, so why not now? It wasn't a smart attitude, but it was one I couldn't help but feel.

One night, staying at another farm in Tuscany, I met the hosts for pizza in a neighbouring village at the end of my day off. There were only three seats in their Land Rover and four of us going back to the farm.

So I did what was by all accounts fairly common here – I sat on the outside, on the bonnet and holding onto the roof rack. Travelling down steep, winding roads I clung on tight, hoping no wild boar or foxes would appear, causing sudden braking. The fear gave me a surge of adrenaline and I loved it, it was like having my very own rollercoaster.

At a hostel in Umbria I took one of the bikes, free for guests to use, out for a spin – only realising, as I dipped down a steep hill at great speed, that the brakes didn't work. Holy fuck! A flash of terror switched to acceptance and I clung on, preparing to crash-land at the bottom. Dust and pebbles spat out from under the tyres as I twisted the handlebars and leant sideways to manoeuvre the corner. I just managed to stay upright as the road flattened again, grazing my foot and ankle. I felt like a wannabe off-road racer and giggled to myself that I'd managed to escape serious injury. And from then on I made sure I only cycled on the flat.

Everything was very ordered in this Tuscan town, very suburban. People would drive everywhere and there was no chitter chatter or kids playing on the streets. No noise at all, in fact, except cars that would come and go from garages, security gates opened and then locked again.

The father ran his daily errands like clockwork and spent much of the time with his vast tool kit in his garage, working on some DIY project or other.

The mother spent her time working away in the kitchen. Cooking, washing dishes, cooking, washing dishes... interspersed occasionally with meeting friends for lunch. I offered to help with chores but she wouldn't hear of it. Meals were served on the dot and if I wasn't there yet I'd hear "Roziieee!" coming from the dining room.

One day I went out for a walk and there was a thunderstorm. I really liked being out in it, it was cooling and also nice having my own space. Walking back to the house, the father pulled up beside me, quite agitated because he'd been out looking for me and got worried.

He was doing it out of a mixture of kindness and having nothing much else to think of. But for the first time on this trip I felt trapped and realised that, with this WWOOF set-up, it's someone else who's in control of your day to day destiny. And here, that made me feel uncomfortable.

As did various conversations with Fabio. The day I arrived we'd stopped at a petrol station and I got out of the car too, for some air. As we waited for the attendant to fill his car, he asked me how old I was.

"You look about 25," he said, eyeing me up and down, and I didn't like the way his eyes hovered around my breasts.

He showed me photos of him years ago and I could see he'd been ruggedly handsome back in the day. He was still clinging onto his amorous youth and I lost count of the number of ex-girlfriends he talked about.

And he was clearly still on the lookout. "You are pretty *and* intelligent," he proclaimed one evening over pizza, as though the two were mutually exclusive. "Just let me know if you are interested in me."

At other farms I met female volunteers who said they'd never in a million years stay on their own with a male host. It hadn't been a prior concern for me; I've always got on with guys as well as I have with girls, and think it is possible to have platonic friendships. That is, if they're cool people.

One day when I was wearing my glasses, Fabio told me off for looking too serious, too "like a teacher".

"It may surprise you to know, but the way I choose to look is not for your benefit," I replied, annoyed and probably sounding a bit prissy. "It's up to me how I look, including whether I wear glasses or not."

He predictably commented when I took a second helping at mealtimes. "You will get so fat in the future!" he'd warn, puffing his cheeks out. It made me take second helpings just to piss him off. I noticed he never said anything when a bloke took more.

Still, needs must, and I kept in mind the WWOOF experience didn't mean automatically becoming best friends with everyone I met. Fabio lacked charm but was an intelligent guy, and we had some interesting conversations about life. I told him about Andrew and said it had for a time made me afraid of life and afraid of death. "Why?" he asked, looking surprised. "But it will make you stronger."

We drove around the region to take in some sights, always stopping for an espresso, and in the evenings visited the local towns, where there seemed to be a *festa* on every night.

I haven't mentioned work at this place, because there wasn't much of it. We did a bit of harvesting but then, after the long summer drought, it rained – starting shortly after I arrived and lasting for days on end. Great for crops but not so much for volunteers needing a purpose.

I cleared out Fabio's workshop-cum-garage and sorted items into boxes, made pear juice and helped his mum make *marmellata di pesche* (peach jam).

I travelled to markets with Fabio, where we set up a stall selling fruit, vegetables, juice and jam. With my lack of Italian we agreed I was of limited use manning the stall, so I went for a wander round the nearby park.

There was a festival on with various street acts performing and bands playing. Of course crazy Pirro, no doubt sensing the opportunity to come and cause mischief, followed me.

He ran up to every dog, no matter what size, checking them out and snarling at them or trying to hump them. He took a real liking to one particular dog near the kids' play park, where the owner's daughter was playing on the swings. The woman asked me if he was mine and I tried to explain he belonged to my acquaintance. I called at Pirro to come but he wouldn't move. I got quite flustered. It was like a parent trying to deal with a kid having a tantrum and looking totally out of their depth.

Eventually I scooped him up, his legs kicking and flailing, trying his best to scamper out of my arms, and took him back to the stall.

Going for another wander later on, I spied Pirro from afar. And then I spied the same mother, looking angry now. I seriously considered turning in the other direction and running, but she clocked me and I walked over. She spoke at me in Italian, fast and incomprehensible. It was like watching a foreign film, when you know, by the action and gestures, what they're *probably* saying but the sound is a babbled stream of words. There was no doubting her anger though. I said sorry and picked the little tyke up and took him back to Fabio, who never thought to have Pirro on a lead. "If he wants to leave, he will leave," he would declare. "I cannot force him to be with me."

Soon Fabio and I got seriously fed up with each other – he had not had a day off for a year, as he kept reminding me. He was tired, and 'having' to pick me up from his parents to go on jobs or trips soon became one thing too many for him. He became grumpy and short with me and, I suspect, my non-interest in him had dented his pride a little.

I felt increasingly unwelcome and trapped. Not only was I staying in someone else's house, but I barely knew them. Our WWOOF 'exchange' was not balanced (though, believe me, I would have jumped at the chance to work) and my so-called host clearly did not want me there. Longing for my own space, I said I was leaving earlier than planned.

Early one drizzly morning Fabio picked me up – looking seriously annoyed that I'd inconvenienced him yet again – and drove me to the train station.

"Ciao. Buona fortuna," he said. "Grazie, ciao," I said, not knowing the Italian for, "I'm sooooooo glad I'm out of here and that I'll never see you again."

I changed trains at Florence and travelled to the north Umbrian town of Umbertide. The landscape was different again, very green. I felt the people had a friendlier air about them, but perhaps my impressions of Tuscans had been tainted by my experience there.

I was on my way to stay with the Millingtons, an English family who rented out holiday cottages near

Umbertide and were looking for help with gardening and maintenance work. I'd found them through HelpX, a scheme similar to WWOOF, which I'd discovered through fellow travellers at a hostel I'd stayed in for a few nights, near Perugia.

It had a similar ethos – exchanging work for a bed and meals – but with a much wider variety of work; as well as farm work, hostel workers, gardeners and childminders were among the roles listed.

Reading the description, and reviews posted by previous HelpX volunteers, I thought my next destination sounded delightful: the name of their home (*Mazzaforte*); the location, high up in the hills overlooking the Niccone Valley; and the thought of a large, bustling household. I was craving some bustle. Still, I was a little nervous – what if it was as disastrous as the previous stay in Tuscany? Would that be my cue to return home? Except, where was home? I didn't really have one.

I arrived at the train station and was met by the youngest son and mum Sally. I liked Sally's no-nonsense English manner, and chatting to her in my native language. There was an ease to it.

After the supermarket we picked up the two daughters from school and drove to the house. On the way up the winding roads, with lush greenery as far as the eye could see, they pointed out a dog by one of the fields. She was called Bianca, a beautiful Maremma sheepdog with a thick white coat. Apparently she had been abandoned and unofficially adopted by neighbours, including the Millingtons. I took to her immediately and we became good buddies during my stay.

The Millingtons were quintessentially English; cut glass accents, Twinings tea, meat-and-two-veg meals, cake for elevenses, three teenage kids who obsessively read the Harry Potter books and were learning Latin at school. (There were four children but the oldest son was teaching English in Asia.)

In fact the mum and dad, Sally and Simon, hadn't lived in England for years and the children were of international upbringing. Japan, Singapore – where Simon worked for a logistics business – and now Italy.

That first afternoon Sally showed me to my room, which was in one of the holiday cottages. They used these to accommodate volunteers out of season and, with the crisp cotton sheets, varnished floors and en suite bathroom, it felt pretty luxurious. We ate soup, salad and sausages for lunch along with the crowning glory: Simon's delicious chilli jam, which would turn out to be my most shared recipe over the next few months.

Splendid isolation. Is that a phrase? It kept coming into my mind while at Mazzaforte. The centuries-old buildings and manicured grounds looked straight out of a photo shoot for a glossy home and garden magazine.

The house was very peaceful, like staying at a retreat. Until mealtimes that is. Dinner was always eaten around the table and served with a glass or two of vino (for the adults), purchased from the local monastery where the shop assistant filled up five-litre plastic containers using a pump attached to the vats, rather like in a petrol station

There would be lively discussions about anything and

everything. The whole family had a great, dry sense of humour – another English trait – and the kids were whip smart. Not least because they must have had to entertain all kinds of HelpX guests, no doubt covering the same conversation ground and repeating jokes, yet they managed to sound engaged most of the time.

Sally and Simon lived by an exact routine: taking their kids to school, walking the dogs, cooking, gardening, ferrying the kids to and from events or meeting friends, and on occasion taking volunteers to festivals.

It felt like I was in safe hands and those few weeks were quite recuperative. I felt welcome there. Not in the full-on, direct way I'd found with Italians; there was a slight distance to it, an English reserve, but with a bit of worldliness thrown in too. After all, they opened their home for much of the year to HelpX-ers from around the globe who, by the sounds of it, possessed all kinds of character traits.

We had interesting discussions about this. How HelpX was perhaps the modern day, technological equivalent of hitchhiking, which they remembered being a popular part of life when they were young; at least with a small band of people willing to take a chance on others.

It was autumn now. Leaves were turning red and orange in the garden and on walks Sally scouted around for edible mushrooms.

They told me this part of Umbria could get grey and drizzly at this time of year, so I felt lucky the sun stayed out most days and the temperature was in the low 20s.

First thing almost every morning there would be blue skies above us and a layer of cloud covering the valley below. I'd never woken to a view quite like it. As the cloud slowly cleared trees and buildings emerged, the rest of the world appearing as the day progressed.

The fine weather meant plenty of gardening work. I cleared thorn bushes and weeds along one of the perimeter fences, cut irises, deadheaded roses, raked up autumn leaves. I again loved being outdoors and doing physical work, the thorn scratches on my hands and arms a sign of a satisfying day's work, though boy did they sting in the shower.

I helped transport newly-delivered firewood from the driveway up to the house; a whole afternoon's work. They had estimated that it would take about 120 trips in all, and while Sally chatted as we loaded the wheelbarrow, Simon growled about it being his most hated job.

He looked like a bear with a sore head as he mechanically stacked each log at the other end, the piles reaching up to well over six feet by evening.

They apologised about the monotony of some of the jobs (see? Very English) but I didn't care. Indeed I was glad to be of use. Besides, the more robotic tasks gave me some thinking time. I took the opportunity to reflect on things, which felt healthy. Some days I felt a loneliness and missed Andrew, other times I enjoyed where I was and what I was doing.

I took the family dogs out on some afternoons – chilled Arctic and boisterous Tarkwa – and apart from the odd hunter we wouldn't encounter anyone for miles. Bianca would join us sometimes, then wander off and appear back at the house later.

Wherever I was doing work in the garden, she would lie down nearby and keep me company. At around 11am I would have my coffee break (with a slice of homemade fruitcake) and sit on the patio terrace and admire the view. Bianca would come, too, and lie in the shade nearby.

One day Sally told me Bianca's companion Pedro (a neighbouring dog) had dropped dead a year or so back, and I could certainly sense a sadness in her. I felt we were similar spirits; like littlest hobos with nowhere in particular to go, and being carried along by the kindness of strangers.

I was so glad I was somewhere I wanted to be – not least because the second anniversary of Andrew's death was fast approaching.

I told Sally about it all and asked for that day off. When it came I got a lift to the train station first thing, via the school run, and bought a return ticket to Assisi.

I'd read this was a must-see town in Umbria. At the hostel I had stayed at on the way to Mazzaforte, fellow travellers had been planning to go for the Feast of St Francis of Assisi, the patron saint of animals and the environment who is honoured around the world in early October.

That was a few weeks ago and now Assisi and its environs had an out of season feel. Nuns outnumbered tourists on the train and the medieval town centre was spacious and quiet and easy to wander round.

At the Basilica of San Francesco I watched the many visitors stand before the tomb of St Francis and trace the sign of the cross. Did their faith provide more comfort after the sudden death of a loved one than the secular soul-searching of an atheist? Or was that faith so severely tested after such an event that it became a burden, weighing down an already addled mind?

In the upper church I sat down in a pew. An obnoxiously loud couple were discussing the frescoes on the wall as though they were at home. Thankfully they left and there was silence, save for footsteps or the swishing of clothes as the odd visitor passed by.

I offered Andrew my own version of a prayer. Then (and I wasn't expecting this, not here) I burst into tears.

Afterwards I wandered through the streets and took in some more sights, and a *pasticceria/gelateria* (cake/ice cream shop) caught my eye. The stone doorway was made up of pillars and intricately carved statuettes, and the window display had rows of meringues, nougat, biscuits and sweets.

Was this the classiest confectionery shop in the world?! It was destined to be part of my Mecca that day, I knew that much. I bought some pistachio nougat, spending most of my weekly budget, and ate it in the nearby piazza, toasting Andrew prior to the first bite.

I had read that Assisi is best enjoyed at dusk but, after people-watching for a while and soaking up the sights within the city walls, I was feeling a bit like an aimless tourist. So, late afternoon I headed for the train, pleased I was returning to the Millingtons.

There are festivals everywhere in Umbria at this time of year. We went to a chestnut festival in Preggio and, on my last day, *Frutti di Bosco* (Fruits of the Forest) in Montone, with two other volunteers who had recently arrived.

With the autumn light, the smell of toasting chestnuts and a slight nip in the air, Montone – another medieval hilltop village – took on a mystical quality. Residents' cellars and workshops had become temporary shop units, selling tantalising wares such as truffle oil, mushrooms, wild berries, cured meats and honey.

We wandered round, taking in the sights and sounds, drank a hot chocolate at the top of the village and meandered back to the car. Then they dropped me off at the station – it was time to head to my next place, an olive farm close to the Umbrian-Tuscan border.

Many of the rural train stations in Umbria have no sign, or only one, so it's easy to miss as the train draws in, especially in the dark. I counted on my timetable how many stops I needed to go. I ticked them off in my head and, I was pleased to discover, caught the right connection to Orvieto.

I arrived at the farmhouse and was shown to my room. It was full with single beds (with clothes strewn across them), dark furniture and paintings of religious icons on the walls. One of them, a portrait of Jesus, stared down at me from the opposite wall when I lay in bed.

A gaggle of volunteers appeared at different times, coming and going between our farmhouse, where we all slept, and the main house, where we ate.

I was sharing the small room with three people, and how different it was from my sparkling, clean holiday cottage at Mazzaforte. But, I realised, this was a WWOOF experience that had to be tried.

I met the hosts but it was clear they did not have as much of a presence as those I'd met on other farms. For one thing they lived in the separate house, for another they did not join us on the daily task of olive picking. We sometimes ate lunch together but at dinner it was volunteers only.

It was the first time I'd volunteered with a group and it was a very different dynamic. Over the weeks it would prove to be energetic, stimulating and so, so funny; and also frustrating and tiring, as very different personalities spent day and night with each other in quite a confined space. That night I chatted to my new workmates: an Austrian, Anna; an enigmatic man of the world, Conrad; two New Zealanders, Matt and Kris; and Tasmin, from Canada.

The next day we headed to the olive grove after a breakfast of spelt bread and honey, coffee and the crispest of apples.

It would become a familiar routine; putting on our wellies and safety glasses (I declined those on the first day as I was wearing my specs); stacking the equipment into the back of the 4x4 truck; jumping in and being driven down to the grove by our foreman Adriano.

The harvesting consisted of lining up nets under trees and zapping the olives from the branches using either machines or handheld plastic rakes.

Volunteers in previous weeks had had the tough job of clearing the land of thorn bushes and weeds so the trees could be accessed in the first place.

Nets were placed under the trees and afterwards rolled up at the end and either side, creating a kind of chute so the olives could be poured into a basket. The baskets were later placed in the truck, taken to the storage shed at the farmhouse then to the local co-op, to be pressed and made into oil.

All fairly straightforward, on paper. But with volunteer workers there are many variables. It was a massive area of land. We had a limited number of nets and different ideas about whether we should work our way up each line of trees, or across.

This caused many heated debates. People using machines always finished first, but needed to wait for the other trees to be finished, and for the nets to be moved across to the next one, before they could start again. There were still thorn bushes all around, so the nets often got caught when being moved.

The land was steep, and our borrowed wellie boots had no grip, so we were always slipping. The first few days I cautiously carried the equipment over the hilly, uneven ground, watching my step.

Towards the end I'd got used to the lay of the land and moved faster and slipped around (sometimes falling on my arse), and it felt as natural as walking in a straight line.

Some of the volunteers listened to music on their music players. Others threw themselves into the task far away from the group, temporarily becoming their own boss.

This first day I worked near Adriano and Anna, who was multilingual and translated for Adriano. She was great to chat to and a similar age to me. While here we became known as Auntie Rose and Auntie Anna; to the other volunteers, who were in their early twenties, we seemed positively ancient.

To be fair, we had a liking for a cup of herbal tea and talk radio (someone once told me those are things you get into in your 30s) but, somehow, we were nearly always the last to bed.

So on my first day on the grove we were chatting away about life when – and I do not know how – an olive branch pinged back and made its way *under* my glasses, and scratched my eye. My actual eyeball. It was *agony*. I took a sharp intake of breath and sat down, clasping my hand over my throbbing, streaming eye, willing the pain to pass.

One of the New Zealanders, Matt, asked if I was alright and came and had a look. I would soon learn he was not one for understatement, as he shouted to Adriano and Anna, in his New Zealand twang, "Oh my fucking god! Have you seen this?! Ros's eye is *fucked!"*

Adriano gave me a lift back to the farmhouse and some eye drops. I wasn't only in lots of pain, but genuinely terrified I was going to go blind.

I lay in the dark, cool bedroom, the sun trying to seep through the net curtains. I left them closed as the dusky light suited my sad thoughts. I willed myself to sleep, hoping I'd wake up and my eye would be miraculously cured (amazingly hopeful, since I'd learned with grief that you cannot simply sleep unwanted things away).

I wished I was still at safe, easy Mazzaforte. Then I wished I was at my mum and dad's house in Edinburgh. The other volunteers returned later and asked how I was. Conrad had managed to hack his thumb with a mini-machete he'd been using; there would turn out to be some injury or other most days here.

They gave me more eye drops, checked if I needed to go to the doctor, and assured me I wasn't going to go blind, something I was still worried about.

And I found their care – these people who I'd met only yesterday – quite nurturing. My eye healed over the next few days, though to this day it is still slightly bloodshot, just to the left of my iris.

We worked hard and we played hard here. For the first week or so I enjoyed it all: working in the sunshine with views of the green terraces and hills beyond, and experiencing a satisfaction at the end when we loaded our day's bounty. But it is mechanical work and does get boring, or would if there wasn't a camaraderie among the group.

When it was dry the routine would be: breakfast, olive grove, lunch, olive grove, break, dinner. Some days it rained and we helped with indoor work; anything from cleaning to translating pages on the website.

Evenings would be spent watching films (I can confirm *Back to the Future* is just as entertaining in Italian) or listening to music in the farmhouse. A couple of nights we went to the snack bar in the nearby village (it was called this in Italian too and therefore pronounced along the lines of "sneckk barrr"). I also enjoyed going out for early evening walks, just as the sky was turning a pinky red. Some nights it rained so hard you got soaked going the few metres from our farmhouse to the main house.

It was all the small moments during this stay that made it memorable. There was quite a cast of characters, who were there for all kinds of reasons.

Matt and Kris were in Europe for two years, heading to London after here to rejoin their band. Matt was a drummer with a twitchy, wired personality and a black sense of humour. He rarely sat still; always stoking the fire or trying to swat flies. Kris was a saxophone player; he had quite a serene quality about him and seemed older than his years. He was funny too. In the afternoons you could hear him practising his sax in the *cantina* (cellar) below the family house, adding what seemed a suitable soundtrack to the mellow autumn vistas beyond.

Tasmin was a smiley, happy-go-lucky Canadian. "Awesome!" was her favourite word. She got drunk very easily and would repeat over and over: "Are you mad at me? Give me a hug!", and do cartwheels down the street. She reminded me of characters from *South Park* and *Glee*, combined and brought to life. And then there was lovely, spirited Anna. I was so glad our paths crossed here, and we are good friends to this day.

Conrad had been travelling for years. He didn't suffer fools gladly and hated small talk. He was thoughtful and principled.

When we were trying to choose music to play I offered him my (admittedly eclectic) MP3 player. People often scoffed at the choice of songs, as it didn't have only 'cool' music on it, and was deemed a rubbish collection by music snobs. Conrad started looking through it. "I'm sure I can find something in here," he smiled, and sure enough he did. Dancing and singing at 1am, to the likes of *Ain't Nobody* by Chaka Khan and *I Think We're Alone Now* by

Tiffany, seemed, at that moment, like the *best* thing in the world.

In this strange universe there were also entertaining people with walk-on parts. Volunteers who came for two or three nights; an ineffectual paid worker who came and was promptly fired after two days; the neighbouring farmer who had a proper, seventies porn star moustache and waved wildly as he drove past.

A guest who was staying with the family joined us for lunch, and was so handsome and had such an aura, all the female volunteers spent much of the lunch just *looking* at him. Needless to say he only ate with us once.

One day we found a dog next to the farmhouse, soaking wet and shivering. We brought him inside and gave him some food and he stood next to the fire. He dried off but still shivered; he was lost and frightened. We made him a little kennel and the family called the phone number on his collar, and two days later he was reunited with his owners.

I would say most WWOOF volunteers bring a surplus of energy to a place, and throw themselves into the work at hand. Harvesting is tough though. At some farms I stayed at, the hosts alternated days so you did hard tasks like clearing land, then, as a break, 'soft' work such as cooking or watering crops.

Here, it was weeks on end of harvesting, and inevitably there was a bit of burnout. During the day "fuck you tree" and "I fucking hate olives!" would travel around the grove.

One day during our break we could hear a cockerel (I

learned the word in Italian for that sound is *chicchirichi!*)
"Would you shut the fuck up," Matt muttered despondently, glancing up from his iPhone. "It's not even fucking morning."

We were burning the candle at both ends, up late drinking wine (€6 for five litres in the village shop – who could resist?), chatting and dancing.

Then, after a few hours' sleep, up for breakfast then to the grove. On the last few days we went to bed fully clothed, ready to get up, clean our teeth and slip our wellies on.

On one of the last nights, when there were only a few of us still at the farm, we went to an olive oil competition. It took place in a village hall, where local producers set up tables with their prize produce, ready to be sampled with bruschetta and a glass of wine.

And then, back at the farmhouse, we partied. We drank and we danced, the sound of the fire crackling its last pieces of wood and music playing on a tinny portable speaker. We attempted rock and roll slides, salsa dancing and Adriano's local dance from back home. At one point a drum and bass track came on and it became a full-on, booze and endorphin-fuelled rave.

When we collapsed into bed dawn had already arrived and, down at the grove, we blinked in the daylight like hungover vampires. And, in defiance of the long-time daily routine, and in response to our tired minds and bodies, we lay down on the massive nets, falling in and out of slumber, having conversations with no boundaries and giggling together like old pals.

That last morning is my fondest memory of this place. Because I won't ever forget how I felt in my heart: truly free for the first time in a little over two years.

SICILY

After a few days in Rome I caught the night train to Sicily. Buying my ticket at the machine, it had offered a choice: men only, women only, or mixed? I didn't really care at that point and just wanted the cheapest option.

Also I had romantic notions of the train to Sicily; a quiet, wood-panelled cabin like something out of an Agatha Christie film (though hopefully no murders); a bar serving coffee or limoncello perhaps.

What was I thinking? It was a night train for the practical purpose of transporting people from the mainland to Sicily, using the special ferry with built-in railway tracks. I was not in tourist Italy now. It was small, no-frills, with bright strip lighting and two bunk beds either side of the cabin.

The first person came in, a suited man in his 40s, who stopped short when he saw me, offering a severe "Buonasera". The next person arrived, a younger, animated guy, who was friendly but on his mobile phone a lot and clearly just wanted to be at his next destination.

Like most people I met, he said he spoke *niente Inglese* then proceeded to speak in passable English. He put my luggage up on the racks and even insisted on making my bed up for me.

In the past I might have thought of this as an Italian machismo. But on this trip I'd seen Italians help people no matter what sex they were, their age, or where they came from. Whereas in Britain our natural instinct is usually to walk on or look the other way, Italians seem to have the opposite reaction and are drawn to helping people out.

This may sound like a generalisation but it's what I witnessed, all over mainland Italy. Driving to an olive press in Umbria we turned a corner and the stacks of crates started sliding, teetering at the edge of the truck, ready to fall. A driver coming the other way saw us. He braked sharply, parked up his Fiat Panda and helped tighten the crates properly with the ropes.

On almost every journey Italians had offered to help me put my luggage up, and in trains where I shared a cabin, they always offered their food and started conversations.

On the way back from Sicily, my bag of oranges (a must-have souvenir) fell on the floor and they all rolled to the other side of the train. The guy whose feet they landed at leant over and calmly bowled them back to me; slowly, one by one, smiling and ending with the usual "Prego!".

Back to the night train to Sicily. I wasn't all that tired, but we all climbed into our beds and I read for a while. At midnight the fourth passenger came in. "Buonasera a tutti," he announced. And then I learned the best reason for requesting a women-only cabin: the snoring. Man it was loud! And all night too. I drifted off but didn't really sleep.

The train shoogled rather than sped through the southern Italian countryside, and it's hard to sleep when shoogling. And my mind had an inbuilt alertness any time a train stopped at a platform, especially in the pitch-black night, which happened a lot on this journey. *Where the hell are we? Is it my stop?! Have I got everything – passport, tickets, farm directions, phone card?*

It was soon morning and I stumbled out of the cabin, clutching my toothbrush and wash bag, looking dishevelled and desperately in need of freshening up.

In the corridor I passed a guy in his 20s, impeccably dressed in the cleanest, fluff-free jumper and trousers, and trainers that looked like they were bought yesterday. Obligatory sunglasses on, leaning forward with his elbows pressed on the ledge below the window, he looked like he'd just joined the train fresh from home, not spent a night on it.

I tried to scurry past him, feeling a little ashamed of my appearance. It was a feeling that had been building since spending the weekend in Rome, looking every inch the northern European backpacker. In my scruffy high-tops, dorky kagoul and with unkempt hair I had watched in awe at the parades of style all around me.

Interestingly, though, it wasn't a snobby atmosphere. In Rome, just as in rural Italy, I found the people to be, on the whole, warm and friendly. They just also happened to have an inbuilt sophistication that meant everyone, young and old, with their padded winter coats, glossy hair and tall boots, looked like they were in a *Tatler* photo shoot.

We finally arrived at Catania and I got off the train, having had approximately 40 minutes sleep. I just wanted to have arrived, but still had to get to Lentini. This is the way with backpacking; when you've arrived at the station there's still a walk, a bus journey or even another train journey to go. And that means orientating yourself in a brand new place – not easy when experiencing a mixture of tired brain, culture shock and a language barrier.

It's times like these I longed for a travelling companion. Someone to chat to and laugh with. Sure, it's a valuable experience travelling solo – I'd recommend it to anyone, to broaden the mind and strengthen the spirit, and to learn who you are. But you can't laugh alone. I've never managed to, not properly. This was why I had joined WWOOF and HelpX, so I had a purpose and a destination, albeit a temporary one.

Next on the list was an orange farm in eastern Sicily, about four miles from Lentini, and knowing that stay was fast approaching was a good feeling.

There were no public toilets at the station so I entered the nearest café, and decided to stay and buy breakfast. I asked if I could leave my backpack at the table and the guy at the till said yes, he would watch it, but with such a demonic smile I spent the whole time in the toilet panicking it wouldn't be there when I got back.

I queued for my precious coffee and pastry – I was so tired and hungry they seemed to turn into gold ingots behind the glass counter. I looked at them longingly and waited to be served.

And I waited, in amongst all the business people having their brisk, stand-up espresso on the way to work. I waited some more then I realised: you pay at the till at the door first, *then* order at the counter.

No-one, staff nor patrons, told me this, they just looked at me with poker faces – and this was the first experience of many where I learned Sicilians have a different way to mainlanders.

Here they were much curter and more distant, and I wasn't sure yet whether this was with tourists or with everyone.

For the next few hours I hung around near the station and didn't explore far, and so my first impression of Catania was that it was nothing more than a scruffy, unfriendly port town, a stop-off point for catching transport to the rest of Sicily. More fool me, I would later discover.

I had exchanged quite a few emails with Elisabetta, an architect and the owner of a farm, Naturamata.

She sounded like a busy, smart woman and friendly, too. She met me at Lentini station and was nothing like I'd imagined – a very youthful face for a start (she looked younger than her mid-30s certainly) and long, wavy black hair. She gave me an inquisitive smile and a firm handshake, and we jumped in to her old-school Land Rover.

I soon saw why she needed a vehicle like this; Naturamata was off road and felt miles from anywhere. We drove along the increasingly bumpy ground and left signs of human life behind, with green hills, red quarries and Mount Etna providing the picture postcard backdrop.

Eventually we arrived at the house, and as Elisabetta parked at the end of the road her two dogs, Leda and Nima, came bounding up. I was so pleased to see there were dogs here because, in one way or another, canine companions had made all my stays complete.

Leda, for the first couple of days, did her guard dog duties and barked when I headed up from the volunteers' house for breakfast. She was lively and lovely and a big fan of cake. Sometimes in the evening, when we were having dessert, the kitchen door would swing open and in walked

Leda, having head-butted it open. The dogs weren't meant to be in the house and her expression showed she knew this – but she would attempt to creep in and lie still under the table, in the hope her behaviour would warrant cake. And she always won.

Then there was Nima, who had the saddest face I'd ever seen. Both dogs often lazed around in the sun and sometimes, after a hard day's graft, I'd walk up the hill to the house and see Nima, resting her chin on her white paws, her big droopy eyes watching me. And she tugged at my heartstrings so much I wanted to cry.

Built on hilly ground, 12-hectare Naturamata was ostensibly an orange farm. There were different types including famous Sicilian varieties such as *tarocco*, plus lemons. People ordered from all over Italy and beyond.

But Elisabetta was working on lots of other projects too, including beekeeping. She – and previous volunteers – had cleared ground to create a kitchen garden. It was such fertile land around here: we picked and ate peas, runner beans, spring onions, avocados, spinach, mint and asparagus, either from the vegetable garden or growing wild. The farmer from up the road brought vegetables and eggs. Most days we made freshly squeezed orange juice; sometimes blood red or the more familiar deep orange colour, but always so tasty and refreshing.

There was no machinery at Naturamata; everything was done by hand. The days here consisted of hacking away at weeds entangling the orange trees, picking oranges, emptying the full baskets into the wheelbarrow and ferrying them through the grove to the pick-up point. Once they'd been driven up to the work shed we spent around two days sorting them for size, making up boxes, packing them, stacking them outside and loading them into the delivery van when it arrived.

We also worked on clearing the terraces of weeds. Elisabetta was hoping to return them to the use for which they had originally been designed: a natural irrigation system, where rainwater flowed down chutes at the end of each terrace.

We watered plants and vegetables, and the steep, uneven land and the size of the farm turned even simple tasks into tough physical labour.

It was a few minutes' walk to the kitchen garden from the water tap, so involved several trips with the wheelbarrow or a pail of water in each hand. For the orange grove we carried a bucket of tools and pickaxes swung over our shoulders, and I always had "*Hi ho, hi ho, it's off to work we go...*" in my head as we set off down the steep paths in single file. The final path was almost vertical and, with slippery grass and grit scattered around, it seemed like pure chance if you made it to the bottom without slipping.

One night I heard the cats moving around outside and a steel grill, which was placed over a hole at the top of the steps up to the main house, being clattered around. The next day I strode up the steps as normal, forgetting the grill had been knocked out of place and when I stepped on it, it bounced up and the sharp edge sliced into my shin. Agony!

My favourite task was packing the oranges into specially designed cardboard boxes, sunlight dappling the workshop and Lucio Dalla playing on the CD machine. I loved the neatness of making up the boxes, fitting the oranges into them (and the soft thud as we shuffled them around to make them fit), closing them, stacking them and stickering them with address labels.

Through the open wooden doors, past the orange groves, I had a view of the sparkling sea. Because I was doing slow-paced work, I had time to appreciate this marvellous place that I currently called home.

A lot of it was hard work and working alone with Elisabetta, I felt I needed to try and keep up with her, which was not likely given she had been running this farm for years.

But she was my only gauge, and she was a whirlwind; clambering up ladders and filling buckets with oranges in what seemed like seconds, chopping vegetables and creating a meal in minutes, baking a three-layered lemon cake in next to no time.

It seemed I had forgotten the wise hare and tortoise fable so pertinent in Piedmont, when I'd worked at my pace and been more productive as a result.

Here I sometimes felt slow and work could feel cumbersome, probably because after months of six-day working weeks involving seriously hard graft, I was tired.

The days took on a routine: breakfast (it was here I learned an espresso, green tea and cake are a great start to the day); four hours' work in the morning; lunch and a siesta; two hours' work in the afternoon.

After that there was the elaborate routine of feeding the four cats. It involved boiling chicken for one of them, who wouldn't eat regular cat food, and waiting for it to cool down while they all hungrily miaowed.

You had to place a security gate across the doorway so they wouldn't scamper into the kitchen. There was even one we christened Spidercat, who tried her hardest to vault over the gate, climbing the mesh vertically and balancing on the thin beam as she worked out how to pounce without being noticed.

Once the chicken was ready you had to walk down the steep hill with it, in the pan of water, the cats and Nema clawing at your ankles.

Keeping Nima outside (her sad face looking more tragic than ever), the next stage involved opening and shutting doors of the outhouse in a sequence, so that the chicken-loving cat was safely in his own, specially made basket and the other cats couldn't steal his tea.

Only then were they allowed through, and through the next door again, where they were fed (in amongst thick nettles, conveniently), pouncing on the food like they'd not eaten for weeks. Then it was time to get the dog food, head outside where Nima was waiting – jumping around now – and take the filled bowls back up to where they hung out, just outside the kitchen.

There were lots of parts of the day like this featuring the idiosyncrasies of Naturamata, which seemed hard to master at first. For example the shower: jump in and run the water just enough so you are wet. Turn the shower off. Apply shampoo and soap. Turn the shower back on, and enjoy the warm water for two minutes until it stops.

In the evenings we cooked in Elisabetta's little kitchen, with music playing in the background. We played cards, she played guitar and sang, or we discussed life and love.

She could be really bossy – or perhaps just very Italian – issuing demands about what to chop next, how often to stir and so on. Towards the end of my stay I lost my grip while carrying the pan (containing the cat's chicken) and scalded my hand. I was so tired I absent-mindedly stared at the boiling water pouring onto my hand, then the searing pain kicked in. I ran it under cold water and told Elisabetta a few minutes later. She gave me a cutting from an aloe vera plant, while at the same time shouting at me for not alerting her straight away, so the medicinal juice could get to work immediately.

But this was the Sicilian way. No holds barred. She could also be fantastic company and we had a good laugh together.

She showed me how to make true carbonara (no cream!) and other tasty dishes, such as pasta with peas, onion and pancetta. I discovered one of my favourite salads here too: blood orange, onion, red chilli and olive oil. It seemed the simpler the recipe the better, not least because the freshly picked vegetables were truly bursting with flavour.

In the middle of my stay Miu arrived. A Japanese photographer who had been living in London, she brought a lovely vibe to the place and was brilliant company. The three of us had a good laugh and worked well together, outdoors and in the kitchen.

After work I often walked up the hill where, after a certain point, Mount Etna came into view. One day in the orange grove I heard what I thought was thunder – in fact it was Etna erupting! This was a fairly regular occurrence, apparently. That night Elisabetta and I climbed the hill and could see streaks of red lava sparking on the side of the mountain.

Early evening I'd go downhill to the orange grove, the green trees touched by a golden light. It was really beautiful, and the only sounds were the river flowing and insects buzzing. On the way I'd pass all kinds of cacti and wildflowers, so varied and colourful it was like leafing through a Dulux paint catalogue.

I got one day off a week, the Thursday, because that is when Elisabetta travelled to Catania to do her architect work. That first day off she gave me a lift to Lentini in her Land Rover at 6.30am, glowering at drivers who stared at her – I think her self-sufficient, tomboy way of life was still quite unusual here.

We caught the train to Catania and she took me for breakfast at her office. Crossing the wide roads just outside the station (as I had falteringly done around a week earlier) she told me, while striding across: "You must go. Nobody will wait for you, it is up to you to stop the cars." And in one fell swoop I learned the rule (albeit a crazy one) about crossing roads in Sicilian cities.

At the office she drew me a map of where to find the good places in Catania, off the tourist trail: clothes markets (where posters tell you everything is 50 cents, so no danger of being fleeced), the best shop for *arancini* (rice balls coated with breadcrumbs), the stretch of sea where office workers take an afternoon dip.

Elisabetta had also arranged for the daughter of her partner to meet up with me. I called in for her at her apartment and she took me to the best *gelateria* in town, where I had my first pistachio ice cream, and then for a ride on her moped.

I had a parcel to send and tried the post office three times. The first time, it was closed even though the opening hours said it should have been open. The second, there was an electricity fault so they closed while it was being fixed.

Finally, it was open. I took my ticket and saw my number was close to being called. But there was one woman serving and her current customer was a good mate by all accounts, and they stood chatting for a good ten minutes, no joke.

I started getting twitchy and irritated, and looked around – all the locals waiting had those poker faces again, and seemed oblivious to having to queue.

But apart from the post office errand taking up too much of the day, I absolutely loved that trip to Catania. Partly because the upside of lots of heavy work days in a row means you really do appreciate your rest day, and feeling in good shape physically meant I had a clear-eyed, positive energy to enjoy it all with.

And partly because it's a fascinating place. Once I got out of the station area (which I'd failed to do when waiting for my connecting train to Lentini), I saw that Catania has all kinds of wonders, from the bustling fish market to Villa Bellini, with snow-capped Etna in the background.

The first few nights I had slept in the volunteers' house, down a pathway from Elisabetta's kitchen and bedroom. The stone walls were home to all manner of beasties and I could hear mice scratching around in the dog and cat food next door.

I used to be terrified of mice and spiders, but I'd grown used to this kind of thing now. At a farm I stayed at in Tuscany I had a wee room with a platform bed. The ceiling, just above, was covered in spiders weaving their webs and many unidentified insects had made their home there too.

While I still didn't like them, I was by now unfazed by these various creatures. However, I didn't like the damp coldness to the air. Perfect for the warm spring, no doubt (in summer it was so hot everyone slept outside), but now it was too chilly.

So after a few days I put my tent up, under the trees, with a view of the deep blue Ionian Sea.

It was common for volunteers to camp here and to use the single beds from the house. Mine fitted in my tent just right. I had camped many times, but mostly in Scottish or Cumbrian rain or drunk at festivals.

Here at Naturamata I learned, at the age of 37, that, if properly tired and so long as your bed is comfy enough, camping is the most wonderful thing! I loved climbing into my cosy nest and knowing, seconds after closing my eyes, I would be fast asleep. The temperature was just right and in the morning I always woke at 6am, no alarm needed thanks to the chorus of birdsong.

Four weeks after arriving at Naturamata I bid a fond farewell to Elisabetta and Miu at Lentini station, and headed for Catania, where I had to catch a bus to central Sicily. Next up was housesitting.

The owner of the house, Vittorio, spent winters in the north of Italy selling aromatherapy oils at markets. He was returning in a couple of weeks and had arranged for his Swiss neighbour, Matthias, to pick me up at the bus station.

We did a supermarket shop and left the village, off the main road onto a track that went through the woods. "That's where you catch the bus to the village, but I don't know how often it is. Or you can hitch," explained Matthias, and I looked woefully over my shoulder as the non-descript stretch of road disappeared behind us.

We drove down a dirt track for what seemed like a long time and arrived at the house. Through the metal gates I saw Lupo lying on the ground. A black guard dog, he looked fierce but as I approached I got a good feeling about him, and loved his bright orange eyes and blonde eyebrows.

Inside the house there was another neighbour, Maurizio, and Paolo, from Palermo, the current housesitter whom I was swapping with. Paolo showed me around the house. It was a mountain cabin with a basic bathroom, living room with platform bed, and kitchen.

"Look me," he said, alternating between English and

Italian, showing me how to work the wood burner and the oven, and how to refill the water tank.

He pointed to a switch. "When you have this on, NO *doccia* [shower], or pfffffffffoowwwwww!" he shouted, demonstrating an explosion. I had to check with him about four times which way was on and which was off, just to be sure, an image of a destroyed mountain cabin already haunting my mind.

I asked Paolo how he had enjoyed it here. He said he was not happy the first two days, because he was all alone and it felt strange. But then he loved it, because he could do anything he wanted.

Paolo, Maurizio and Matthias left and I felt excited. I had a house to myself and it was true, I could do ANYTHING I wanted.

I cooked some food and sat outside the cabin in the sunshine. I started reading *In Sicily* by Norman Lewis (a captivating book) and stroked Lupo, who was curled up beside me, looking like an oversized teddy bear. And I felt quite content.

The first night and second day it rained and rained. I lit the wood burner, remembering how as a kid, my dad had shown me how to make firelighters out of concertinaed newspapers, and stack kindling like a mini wigwam.

Massive, joyous flames leapt up, giving light and much needed heat... only for it to dwindle and die a few minutes later. I tried again and the same thing happened. It was so disappointing it made me cry. But third time lucky!

Just as the cabin started heating up, the chimney flue,

which went from the wood burner through the roof and outside, started leaking. I put a pan under it and hoped it would miraculously stop.

The lashing rain continued and the view outside had gone, replaced by a curtain of mist and a chilly breeze. Sicilian winters weren't meant to be like this! Not in my mind anyway. I may as well have been back in Scotland on a dreich January day.

I had loved the *idea* of living here with no technology. But who was I kidding? My mobile phone unexpectedly had an excellent signal, and I'd long been programmed into the "Query? Google it!" way of thinking.

And so I Googled *wood burner chimney leaks,* as you do, and the results glared back: "Danger of wood burners" then "Death due to faulty wood burner" which then led to "Carbon monoxide poisoning". Carbon monoxide poisoning!! That's the one where there are no signs, right?

I read on. "If you develop any nausea or flu-like symptoms which are relieved while outside, call the emergency services," the internet instructed. So I tried this out – and felt nauseous and a bit dizzy, even after stepping outside.

It also said some people don't get symptoms, they just never wake up. Well I *had* always favoured the instant, painless kind of death, I told myself, trying to put a positive spin on things as usual.

I wedged the front door open, got into bed and piled the blankets over me, the smell of old smoke still quite heavy in the air. *I should think some final thoughts, perhaps?* I wondered, but was asleep almost straight away.

The next morning I was surprised to wake up. And I was still worried. How long could it be before carbon monoxide poisoning took effect?

I phoned Maurizio and said I would try to speak Italian, which was fine – I had already noted down the words for chimney and leak – but understanding his replies was hard. I got that he said he would come by later, at around 2pm, and when he arrived he was unfazed. He said the leak was caused by the heavy rain, it was nothing to worry about.

Oh to be as unfazed as that. Instead my mind mulled over massive questions about our existence. Ever since Andrew's death I had had a fear of dying; I had wondered which way I would go and whether I would be young too. If carbon monoxide poisoning was not to be my fate, what would be?

And what is fate anyway? I'd always held a belief that it plays an important role in life. I saw it as things happening for a purpose, of life working out for the best. Fate makes things fit and feels comforting, even if its workings are not always immediately apparent.

I'd lived in unhappy flatshares, had jobs I hated and relationships that had ended, leaving me devastated at the time... but then something wonderful would happen, something that couldn't have happened had I not taken a certain path previously.

So all these things were fated to happen, and that is how I am here now, I'd think. I'd feel thankful that I'd learned and I'd grown from the experience, and that life seemed to be back to its recognisably enjoyable, rhythmic state.

How laughable this way of thinking now seemed. I had learned, in the starkest of ways, that there is no design for life, and that we have absolutely no idea what is around the corner. Life is not easy nor kind and the fact I had thought it could be – if you treated others well and did good things – now seemed totally absurd. It also showed how lucky I had been until one autumn night in 2010.

That life is so chaotic it can change at any minute was a brutal truth. I had reacted to this with a *what will be, will be* attitude in mainland Italy, and reaped the rewards.

Now, alone in the middle of the Sicilian wilderness, I was again scared by life and continued wrestling with ideas about fate and my purpose.

Twice a day I took Lupo out for long walks through the woods. What a lovely, lovely dog. He was physically big and boisterous, yet walked by my side and waited patiently as I unpadlocked gates and locked them again, never pulling at the lead. There were rain showers and sunshine and we walked past green fields with purple and pink wildflowers.

It being the tail end of winter, there were no outdoor tasks to get on with. Perhaps if I was an instinctively rural person or a seasoned housesitter I'd have created tasks, but instead I stuck to what I knew.

I did a lot of writing. I collected wood. I cooked. I did an online Italian course. I worked my way through the English language novels on the bookshelf. I wrote letters to my mum and read and sent emails on my phone – I relished this link to the outside world.

Matthias called and said he would come up to show me the way to his house. He lived down the hill, where he and his wife grew vegetables, made olive oil and kept goats. To get there involved cutting through the woods. We zigzagged through the dense trees. "You take the path that is clearest, do not go too far up or too far down," Matthias said matter-of-factly in his Swiss-German accent.

I thought of Hansel and Gretel and wished I'd brought something with me to mark the path. "From the large tree," he continued a few minutes later, pointing at one that looked the same as the other trees all around it, "you go down, towards the pine tree."

I knew I would not find my way back and got increasingly worried as we sat in his kitchen drinking coffee. My biggest fear was getting disorientated and totally lost, going round in circles, panic rising.

Had this guy not seen *The Blair Witch Project*?! When they realise they've gone in a circle and are back at the same part of the woods is, to my mind, one of the most terrifying film scenes ever.

When it was time to head back I asked Matthias to show me. "I can try, but my mind works in strange ways and I don't have a good sense of direction," I explained, wondering why I'd decided to do housesitting in the middle of nowhere.

I lead the way and tried to turn up at a first, smaller pine tree, then could not work out which way to go. *Do not go too far up or too far down* rang around my head. But too far up or down from what? I needed landmarks, and there weren't any.

Matthias took me along the route until I could see the roof of my cabin in the distance. I was so scared it was going to disappear from view I didn't take my eyes off it.

I was so pleased to get back, and sat with Lupo in the sunshine. And for the next couple of days I tried to make the most of this mountain sanctuary. But while I enjoyed walks with Lupo, I started to hate the padlock on the gate on the way back down to the house. I fumbled with the lock and often dropped the bunch of keys – it was like my instinct was telling me I really didn't want to be locked in for the night.

Although I was in a place of beauty, my heart felt empty. It was all wonderful if you wanted to find yourself. But I didn't want to find myself. At that precise moment in time I just wanted to wolf down pizza and coke. Pizza and coke!

I found it boring continually cooking and eating on my own, alternating between pasta and couscous with passata. When I visited the stunning Villa Romana del Casale, a week or so later, a Sicilian recipe book on one of the tourist stalls outside caught my eye. On the blurb it said: "Cu mancia sufu s'affuca" – he who eats alone chokes himself. Exactly! That's one of the things I'd loved about Italy, the communal dinners.

I felt homesick for… where? I didn't know. Those last few months in Carlisle I couldn't wait to leave, and would have loved the thought of housesitting in the Sicilian wilderness. I missed various WWOOF volunteers and hosts I'd met, but had always felt it was the right time to leave each farm.

The strange thing here was that, even though on paper I was free as a bird, in reality I wasn't. I felt trapped. I couldn't get to the village without Matthias (I didn't want to hitch and couldn't find any online information about buses to the village), but I couldn't get to his house through the woods. I would, very definitely, get lost.

If you smoke you need to know you can get cigarettes from somewhere if you run out. You need to know that for peace of mind, even if you still have nearly a whole packet of cigarettes. This was like being too far from a cigarette shop. It made me feel angsty.

I have a friend who loves living in London for its choice of cultural events. In fact she rarely goes to the theatre or concerts or exhibitions – but that's not the point. The point is *she could if she wanted to*. And so it was with this housesitting gig; I would have felt far more comfortable knowing I could nip to the village, to civilisation, *if I needed to*.

When there's not a soul around and no-one to distract you, man your mind can wander. I'd already panicked about carbon monoxide poisoning and a re-enactment of *The Blair Witch Project* in the middle of those goddamn woods. And next? Robbers, of course.

Matthias had mentioned that robbers were a problem in the area and a big reason for people having housesitters, as well as to look after their pets. He said robbers had got in through the roof of Vittorio's cabin a couple of years ago. That night I could not sleep. I lay in the dark and listened to Lupo barking outside. *Normally he is more peaceful. Does he know something I don't, in a Lassie-style way?* I thought, cowering under my downy. Then every crack of light looked sinister, every shadow.

My imagination was running riot and I made myself scared stiff, too frightened to get up and turn the light on.

"Okay, so THIS is how it ends for me. I get it! Just make it hurry up!" I told whoever was in charge of my fate that night (my mind still stubbornly clinging onto that idea of a certain fate).

Sleep was out of the question so I sat up and played computer games in the dark, glaring at the screen like a frustrated teenager, building a wall between me and the outside world.

I got up after a couple of hours' sleep. It was raining heavily outside and, as I put my wellie boot on, I felt something. I took it off and shook out a squished cockroach, and saw spots of insect blood on the sole of my tights. I sat down to breakfast for one.

"Buon appetito," I said, by now feeling very sorry for myself.

Later that morning Matthias phoned to say his wife Katrin was back from Switzerland, and would I like to come down for lunch. Yes please!! I headed to the top of the woods where he came and met me, in his yellow sou'wester.

At the house Katrin greeted me warmly and invited me in, giving me some Birkenstocks to wear inside. They had a friend staying from Switzerland and the kitchen had an appealing busyness to it, with food being prepared and water boiling on the stove.

Katrin spoke excellent English but I asked if I could attempt to converse in Italian. She readily agreed, and because she was so nice I didn't feel like an idiot, as I had with some people, and felt I could at least try.

We ate pasta, local sausage (apparently each butcher has his own speciality, using different herbs and spices) and artichokes. With the latter I'd only ever come across the hearts, but these were the whole vegetable.

I started carving away at the leaves with my knife and fork, glanced up and saw Matthias looking at me curiously. "Eh, we do it different," he said, and demonstrated the right way: peeling off one leaf at a time, squeezing on some lemon juice, and nibbling the soft leaf until you get down to the coarse end, which you leave on your plate.

With conversation, a long lunch and a glass of wine, it was a lovely afternoon. I felt quite sated. Towards the end I asked if they were going into the village in the next day or two, as I needed to get some supplies at the supermarket. They weren't, but went to the fridge and larder and returned with Dolcelatte, bread, fruit and chocolate.

When I headed back to the house Katrin and her friend accompanied me and we had a cup of tea outside the cabin.

They had brought lots of yellow tape and when I went for a walk later I saw it tied round trees every few feet on the route to their house, the plastic ribbons blowing in the breeze and bringing a happiness to my heart.

I felt lighter than I had in a while; because I could now find my way to their house, if need be, and because it demonstrated once again the kindness of strangers.

Vittorio was due back a few days before I was due to leave, but phoned to say his ferry from Genoa was delayed because of the stormy weather.

He finally arrived at 3am. Lupo knew and started barking quite a few seconds before I heard the sound of a car driving down the steep road.

Tall and trim, Vittorio looked very smart in his jumper and waistcoat and seemed wide awake. I admired his spirit, his ability to travel almost 48 hours from Como to

Palermo (including delays) with little complaint.

Over breakfast I told him about previous farm experiences and about Andrew. How life had changed completely from one day to the next; that now I was on Part 2 of my life but didn't know where I would end up.

He asked me how I had got on here and I said, honestly, I was craving city life. "You want to go to an art gallery to look at pictures of nature, when here it is all around you," he laughed.

Vittorio was one of those people who didn't eat for a day or more and it didn't seem to bother him. He didn't get hungry or grumpy, he seemed to thrive on it. He was very virtuous, extolling the wonders of nature, the benefits of a pure diet. When I put milk in my coffee he looked aghast.

We were coming from opposite ends of the spectrum, really. I had cabin fever and was in transition. He had returned home after months away, but couldn't settle back in with a nomadic housesitter there.

That last night I was so tired and happy to be leaving the next day, I slept really well. We were out of the house by 8.30am and after a fortnight (was it only a fortnight?) of isolation I made up for lost time, visiting Villa Romana del Casale and the nearby town, Aidone.

On the way through the forest two young, chubby guys drove fast towards us and as they passed, Vittorio asked them to stop and spoke to them in Italian. They looked sheepish, smiling uncomfortably.

Afterwards Vittorio explained he'd told them to take it easy driving through the forest and asked them if they were going jogging (the forest was popular with joggers) and they said yes. He had replied: "Good, you look like you need to."

"There is one rule in Sicily – and that is that there are no rules," Vittorio had declared as we entered the town. After stopping at a garage to proudly show his mechanic his new car, we stopped at the *panificio* (bakery) for bread, which turned out to be closed.

Then to the sports bar for a cappuccino, where I also had a *cornetto con crema* (like a custard-filled croissant). "You want to line your stomach with this artificial stuff?" Vittorio asked, dismayed. "Yes!" I replied. I really did.

We visited another panificio, where there was a crate of ruby red oranges at the door and Vittorio asked if we could sample a couple. The owner appeared from the back, wearing a white apron, sweating and smiling. "Buongiorno," he grinned and told us to help ourselves.

Cloud was rolling in and against the pale yellow buildings there was a muted, ghost town feel. Almost every street had a poster for a soon-to-be visiting circus – the highlights being a white tiger and the biggest hippopotamus in the world.

I had a parcel to pick up and we went to the post office: closed. A handwritten sign saying 'Chiuso' had been hastily taped onto the door. There were policemen standing around the back – apparently it had been broken into during the night.

Vittorio asked a member of staff if he could find my parcel, explaining I was leaving today. After some persuasion they agreed and a few minutes later Vittorio appeared victorious, the parcel under his arm.

We continued on up the hill to the historic town centre. The mist was beginning to clear and at the bottom of wide steps, at the foot of one of the many churches, stood a man in his 50s, wearing a long wool coat and sunglasses, cigarette in hand, puffs of smoke floating up to the sky. He looked like an extra in a 1930s film.

We sat outside the *duomo*, the cathedral, drinking Campari. The barman free-poured them and it was a huge measure.

By the time I got on my westbound bus, at midday, I felt a little tipsy, a feeling no doubt added to by the bus speeding through the lush landscape, my unopened birthday parcel sitting on my knee (I liked prolonging the surprise), and the prospect of exploring Palermo.

I booked my apartment using the internet on my phone and after a couple of hours we arrived at the bus station.

The first thing I noticed was how different the air was. There was no misty mountain chill here but instead a city heat, and I had to peel off two layers.

I felt so excited. Palermo was busy and chaotic, vibrant and unpredictable. I was still on my own, yet I didn't feel lonely.

After checking into my apartment I wandered round the side streets filled with bustling market stalls, along the slippery marble pavements, past grand theatres and columns, buildings old and new.

Mopeds and cars sped by, drivers taking no notice of keeping in lane, and rarely stopping at zebra crossings or traffic lights.

When I picked up a map, the man at the tourist info kiosk asked where I was from and enthusiastically babbled about his love of Irvine Welsh and his loathing of nuclear power. Why did we still have nuclear power stations, he wondered? We should all be protesting – look what happened in Japan.

I walked along the packed streets. As the evening sky filled with pink clouds, painting that magic light you get in port cities, I felt like I was moving with time again.

That night I bought red wine, a coke and a takeaway pizza. I took them back to my apartment, just up from the famous *Quattro Canti* (four corners), and felt deliriously happy.

I sat on the double bed and munched through my feast, including French Fancies for dessert. These had been in the parcel Vittorio had collected for me at the post office, sent by a friend in Edinburgh.

They were a bit squashed and as sweet a taste as you could find, and all the more glorious for that – I felt like I was sinning against the church of the holy countryside.

On the second day I went exploring. It was muggy again and as I walked down Via Roma, traffic roaring past and spewing fumes into the air, I saw people walking up from the station, lugging suitcases. They looked lost and confused, the question "Have we made a terrible choice coming here on holiday?" etched on their faces.

I discovered shopkeepers were mostly rude and was always told tourist prices when I asked how much things cost. My beginner's Italian was far from perfect but sufficient for basics like buying tickets and shopping.

In one convenience store, where the shopkeeper charged me more than €5 for a small bottle of water, a coke and an apple, I got really annoyed.

"Cinque euro per questo? Io sono un turista, ma io non sono stupida!!" (€5 for this? I am a tourist, but I am not stupid!!) I said, sing-songing the words and taking on the spirit of an animated Italian.

A group of boys came into the shop and listened. "Cinque euro è troppo costoso, no?" (€5 is too expensive, isn't it?) I asked. "Si, é vero!" (Yes, it's true!) they chorused. The shopkeeper agreed to go down to €2.50.

I bought bread at various neighbourhood panifici (my favourite was called Panificio Il Grano D'oro, where it was around 60 cents for a freshly baked loaf) and cheese and ham at the market. I ate lunch in the various parks, read my book, relaxed and people-watched.

I ticked off the tourist list; visiting the botanical garden, the catacombs and the cathedral at Monreale. But mostly I relished just wandering around, marvelling at this city where every corner seemed to breathe life.

I loved the idea of travelling round Palermo by motorbike and, as luck would have it, the apartment owner offered to take me out on his.

We cruised through the city, to Mondello beach, where we ate ice cream hamburgers (two huge scoops inside a brioche bun – so wrong it seemed very right), and further out along the coast. It was thrilling racing up and down winding, woodland roads and a brilliant way to see the area.

It was a day or two later I noticed it missing. My falcon necklace, the one piece of jewellery I had taken away with me. I hunted around the apartment room before checking out, and at first I felt upset that it was gone, and a bit lost without it.

Perhaps someone was now wearing it, perhaps it had been scooped up like rubbish and was sitting in some dusty tip somewhere in Sicily.

But my favourite thought was that it had made its way into the sea, a glistening jewel carried by the waves and meeting Andrew's ashes somewhere.

On my final afternoon in Palermo I sat at the port and felt the warmth of the sun on my face. I listened to the hustle and bustle and watched city life go by. I had no plans for after here but I didn't feel afraid now. Because I knew that despite, no, *because* of what had come before, I could take the world on.

We all can.

Acknowledgements

Andrew, thank you for the pleasure-filled days. For seeing the magic, for making me laugh and feel so cared for.

Mum, I really enjoyed sharing my Italian adventures with you, by email and Skype, but most of all by letter. I wish you were here to receive your signed book. You would have got the first copy.

And thank you to:
My family and friends in Cumbria, Edinburgh, London and beyond, for being there with tons of love and support, not just in the dramatic early days but for a long time after. I trust you know who you are.

Andrew's family, for your warmth and kindness.

Troy Slater (www.troyslater.com), for my painting.

Hosts in Italy, for the warm welcomes and experiences I won't forget.

Beth, Fiona and Ruth, for your wise words and support.

And last but not least. Thank you Alex, Caroline, Chris, Emily, Kath, Roger and Vicky for help in various book-related ways (and helping me stay sane!): reading the draft, useful feedback and encouraging comments, proofreading, techie assistance, publishing suggestions, emergency printer provision (and special thanks to Emily, for all of these things).